HAPPENS EVERY DAY

An All-Too-True Story

Isabel Gillies

SCRIBNER

New York London Toronto Sydney

SCRIBNER
A Division of Simon & Schuster, Inc.
1230 Avenue of the Americas
New York, NY 10020

This book is a work of nonfiction. Some names and other details, however, have been changed.

First Scribner hardcover edition March 2009

For information about special discounts for bulk purchases, please contact Simon & Schuster Special Sales at 1-800-456-6798 or business@simonandschuster.com.

DESIGNED BY ERICH HOBBING

Text set in Bembo

Manufactured in the United States of America

1 3 5 7 9 10 8 6 4 2

Library of Congress Control Number: 2008051362

ISBN-13: 978-1-4391-1007-2
ISBN-10: 1-4391-1007-7

For my boys

HAPPENS EVERY DAY

1

One late August afternoon in our new house in Oberlin, Ohio, my husband, Josiah, took it upon himself to wallpaper the bathroom with pictures of our family. Over the years, we had collected an enormous number of framed pictures. Some were generations old and really should be called photographs; like the one of Josiah's grandfather, a Daniel Day-Lewis–like, strong-looking man, sitting in profile on a porch, casually surrounded by all his family, including my father-in-law, Sherman, at age ten. I always thought that picture would have been a good album cover for a southern rock band like Lynyrd Skynyrd. There was one of my great-grandmothers looking beautiful, rich, and Bostonian on her wedding day in 1913. There was a picture of my mother sitting on stairs at Sarah Lawrence College in Jackie O sunglasses and pigtails. Numerous black-and-white pictures of various family dogs.

My grandparents on my mother's side always had somewhere between two and six black labs around at any given time. There were also two St. Bernards, one named

McKinley and the one before that, Matterhorn. They lived in Croton, New York, on the Hudson River, on Quaker Ridge Road and belonged to that John Cheever group of eccentric intellectuals that had a little extra money, mostly from prior generations, and a lot of time on their hands. My grandparents and John Cheever used to write letters to each other in the voices of their Labradors. Seriously. My grandfather had the mother, Sadie ("one of the great Labradors," he would say in his Brahmin accent), and Mr. Cheever had the daughter, Cassiopeia. Dogs are important in my family. But in addition to dogs my grandparents also had a raccoon, Conney, who would sit on one's shoulder during drinks and beg for scotch-coated ice cubes; a toucan; a sheep named Elizabeth; and, for a short time, two lion cubs. It sounds like they were vets or they lived on a farm, or they were nuts, but really they just loved animals and birds. The house that my mother grew up in was big and white with lots of lawn. They had a mimeograph in the living room that my grandmother Mimi knew how to operate and, as a family, they created *The Quaker Ridge Bugle,* which was later printed as a little local paper. My grandmother was an artist. She mainly painted and drew birds. My brother Andrew and I now have them on our walls. I remember her as very beautiful but thin. She wore long braids and black socks with sandals. She and my grandfather, who was a photographer among other things, lived in Guatemala later in their life, so I remember her shrouded in lots of brightly colored striped ponchos. In her day, though, she looked like a fey Katharine Hepburn. Like my grandfather, she was from a nice old American family. She was an odd bird. She was an intellectual, a good writer of letters, and also was probably one of the first anorexics. She rebelled against her aristocratic, proper upbringing as much as she could by becoming an artist and leading a somewhat alternative life filled with books and chaos. She spent many hours in her studio alone, away from her children, whom she didn't really know what to do with. My mother, the eldest, ended up running the show a bit, which is probably why she is such an organizational dynamo now. "It sounds a little looney, and it was," my mother says.

Among the pictures Josiah hung on the bathroom wall was one of my father shaking hands at an Upper West Side street fair when he ran for New York City Council in 1977. He didn't win the election, but my memory of that is not as strong as my memory of his photograph plastered on the front of the Eighty-sixth Street crosstown bus that I took to school. I'll never forget the image of my father bounding toward me, his hand strongly gesturing forward, as I got out my bus pass. ARCH GILLIES CITY COUNCIL AT LARGE. I thought he should have won. As far as I am concerned my father really should have been the president of the United States. He can see the big picture and he is fair. His grandparents were Scottish immigrants. His parents were of modest means but made a sturdy, dependable, nice life for their only son in Port Washington, Long Island. My grandfather was in the navy, and by hook or by crook, having never gone to college, he made his way up the ranks to rear admiral. When he found himself surrounded by other high-ranking officers he learned that they had all gone to something called boarding school. So he came home on leave one day and told my grandmother that they would only have one child, my father, and he would go to school at a place called Choate, a school in Connecticut where a colleague had gone. So my father, who thought he would do what all his other friends did, work at La Guardia Airport, was sent to Choate, which led him on a very successful path. His life took a different turn. He went on to Princeton, where he was on the student council and president of all the eating clubs. He helped change their policies so that all students were eligible to join the eating clubs. He has run things ever since. My parents met on Rockefeller's 1968 presidential campaign. He was the finance director and my mother was the office manager. At the end of the long days they would have a drink in the office together. "I had the scotch and she had the rocks," he would say as he gave my mother a wink.

Also among the sea of photographs was a snapshot of Josiah and his brother, ages four and five, leaning against their father, who was driving somewhere in the South—not a seat belt on anyone. There was another of Josiah's mother, Julia, holding hands with her husband, John, Josiah's stepfather, whose other hand was linked in a chain with four children. One of the children was an eight-year-old Josiah. They were walking across a lawn in Palm Beach in crisp white shorts and brightly colored Izods. Everybody matched.

There were old framed Christmas cards from both of our families—lots of gangly, long-haired boy and girl teenagers standing in front of various mountains in Georgia and on rocky beaches in Dark Harbor, Maine. Both of us have parents who had been married more than once, so we both have an array of step and half and real siblings that we love very much. The titles that came before the word *brother* or *sister* never mattered much.

There was a black-and-white picture of my girlfriends from high school at a Grateful Dead show in Providence, Rhode Island. The slightly curved picture in the frame gave away the fact that I had developed it myself in a photography class at RISD. And there was one of Josiah in a crew shell at his boarding school looking focused. Josiah often made fun of the fact that he was positioned in the middle of the boat to serve as weight, the "meat," rather than being placed in the front as the coxswain, the "brains" of the boat, who navigates the race. Out of the eight rowers, though, Josiah was the one who stood out. When someone in the picture looks like Adonis, it's hard not to notice.

There was a large silver framed picture of me and Josiah walking down the aisle on our wedding day. We got married at Christmastime. I wanted the wedding to feel like a New York Christmas party, so there were paperwhites everywhere. We ate chicken potpie and coconut cake. And then there were many, many photographs of our three boys. Josiah had a son, Ian, from his first marriage, whom I met when he was three. Ian lives in Texas with his mother and is the spitting image of Josiah, dark curly hair and almond eyes that remind me of a sparrow. My favorite picture of him is in black and white and was taken on a pristine beach in the South. It's almost annoying it's so beautiful, but he is wearing a T-shirt with a fierce shark on it that makes the whole thing palatable. Josiah and I have two boys, Wallace, age three on the day that Josiah was bathroom decorating, and James, who was sixteen months old. Both names were in our family trees, but Wallace we came to because we were watching *Braveheart* while I was pregnant. Like I said, I am Scottish. The boys are fair, their coloring more like mine. Josiah is dark. I think of Wallace as the sun: bright, vibrant, and warm and James as the moon: round, steady, and funny. James even likes colder baths. Wallace, like me, wants to be scalded.

We had been hauling all these pictures around with us in boxes. One reason for that was because Josiah was an English professor and we had moved from one college town to another for a number of years. The other was because we were both pretty big WASPs and in our worlds it was looked down upon to have too many beautiful pictures of one's own family ostentatiously displayed in frames around the house. My mother said it was okay to have small framed pictures on your personal desk (she gets everything printed in 3 × 5), but anything more than that was showy and, as she would say, "too much." I always felt sort of sad about this, that there wasn't more evidence of our happy family around for people to see—but I never questioned it. Most of the advice and direction my mother gives I take, but there are a few things I have thrown in the garbage. The picture thing I followed like a good girl, but my mother also thinks cars should be spotless; I like mine to look like my purse. She has shoe polish in brown, black, cordovan, and white and all the brushes and flannels to use them. I have never bought a can in my life. Josiah felt the same way as my mother did about framed pictures. He thought it was embarrassing and silly to take up space with big goopy silver frames filled with frozen happiness, so that he did what he did in the bathroom was mind-blowing.

I am from New York and Josiah is from Florida, where his mother and stepfather lived, and Georgia, where his father and stepmother lived. And although he feels like a northeastern guy, mostly because he went to boarding school in New England at age thirteen, actually he is 100 percent southern.

We were living in Oberlin, Ohio, because Josiah was teaching poetry at the college. Oberlin is a funky, tiny, political, young hot spot in the middle of northeast Ohio that vibed New York City to me a lot because most of the students who went to Oberlin College were from the East Coast if not New York City itself. But it was in Ohio—and it was rural and it was minuscule. A faculty member said that in the summer, when the students were gone, it felt like living in Central Park with no people—and that was kind of right. For the record, I absolutely loved it.

We had gotten the job (in academics you end up saying "we" even if it actually isn't "we," because you move around so much together from job to job that one person slowly loses his or her identity) right after I gave birth in Cambridge, Massachusetts, to our son James Thacher. Because of our chaotic life with a two-year-old, a newborn, a dog, and two cats, I ended up not going out to Ohio to check it out before we moved. I had faith in my dream of a bucolic, happy, secure, academic life. It's a great, great dream if you have it in your head right. Here's what was in my head. I had married a very good-looking (think Gregory Peck), brilliant (most people hate the word *brilliant* to describe a person, but I frankly can't think of any other word to do it—at our wedding Josiah's best friend described his brain as a cathedral) childhood friend that I had re-met at his sister's wedding in Maine. As six- and seven-year-olds we had sailed in little bathtub boats on the Penobscot Bay together, but at the time of his sister's wedding he was getting his Ph.D. in poetry at Harvard and I was being a New York girl in New York. I had not seen him in fifteen years. He was Heathcliff with an earring. It sounds romantic to be married to an actual poetry scholar, but truthfully he never recited poetry to me much or wrote me a poem. It's hard to admit, but I don't really like poetry or jazz. I just don't get it a lot of the time. If someone (and Josiah once in a blue moon would do this) teaches me through every line of a poem I can get it, but it's rare that it hits me in the gut the way a Rolling Stones song does, or the unfinished *Pietà* that I saw in Florence when I was fifteen. Right at the start of our love affair he did give me one of the only poems I do recognize as sublime, a John Ashbery poem called "At North Farm."

Somewhere someone is traveling furiously toward you,
At incredible speed, traveling day and night,
Through blizzards and desert heat, across torrents, through
narrow passes.
But will he know where to find you,
Recognize you when he sees you,
Give you the thing he has for you?

We fell in love in two hours at that wedding on a rare night so foggy it felt like when I was a girl in the 1970s, when it seemed to be foggy all summer. Maine has lost a lot of its fog.

The day after Sarah's wedding was the same day that Princess Diana died in a car crash in Paris. I had hardly slept during the night. I think sudden love fills you with adrenaline, making it impossible for your body to function properly. I heard the news of the princess's death in the morning, but because of my giddy excitement about Josiah, I didn't give myself a chance to take in the sad news until a few hours later when I drove over to meet him for a walk. When I was paused at the stop sign at the end of our road, a wave of grief came over me and I cried for Diana. She was so young, but just that much older than me that I was always taken by her, like you are with your very best, prettiest babysitter. It didn't even occur to me then that she had such small children. Sixteen years earlier, my mother and I had gotten up at four in the morning to watch Diana and Prince Charles get married. When she died she was at the start of something new, like I was then.

For those first three days of September, Josiah and I walked and sat on the beach for hours and talked about what had happened during the years we had missed each other. (It turned out that during his twenties he avoided many summers in Maine. His first wife didn't like it up there so much.) He cooked salmon for me one night and mushroom pasta another. Salmon and mushrooms are the only two foods in the world I don't like. I confessed to him I wasn't nuts about salmon, wanting to be honest, but the next night I ate the mushrooms, not wanting to seem fussy. We went sailing in his parent's 12 (a small, pretty wooden boat) and kissed every chance we got. When it was time for us to go back to our lives, we sat on the rocks at the ferry dock with our datebooks and a thermos of tea Josiah had brought. We planned every single weekend of the upcoming fall. One weekend he would drive down in his white Subaru station wagon to New York. (I was living in Williamsburg in an apartment that had the largest rosebush in the United States. The curator of the botanical gardens came to prune it himself it was such a treasure.) And the next I would take Amtrak up to Cambridge to stay in his apartment, where he allegedly had roommates, though I never met them, and four cats, whom I did meet. I was casually dating an architect, but Josiah told me to stop immediately because I was his now and he was mine. I was flooded with love. He was forceful ("I am going to make you dinner tonight and then we will play Scrabble"; "I will call you at two thirty and if you aren't there I'll try every minute after until you are") and passionate—we had sex for the first time on a rocky beach in the middle of the day. He was a better cook than I am, and when he was ready to serve the meal, the kitchen was almost spotless. At twenty-eight, he had been married and divorced already, something that should have been a red flag, but instead I saw him as fearless and romantic.

He and his first wife, Samantha, were married right out of Yale, so young that it was easy for me to write it off as a mistake. I even ignored the red flag that he had left her *when she was pregnant* to fool around with Edith the weirdo (who ended up plaguing me throughout our marriage). His wife moved to her family's house in Dallas, where she stayed, had the baby, divorced Josiah, and later married a really nice lawyer with white hair. Josiah went religiously every month to see his son. It all felt a tad complicated, but it didn't matter to me because I knew how much he loved me. He was nuts about me. It was one of those times that you feel no need to eat, but do together constantly in sexy restaurants, making out after until they close. I felt suddenly grown-up. He knew me everywhere. He knew me at every time of my life. He knew my parents and I his for our entire lives. I felt seen and understood and accepted. He said he wanted to be by my side forever and there was nothing I could do that would ever make him go away. I had met the man I was to have a big, big future with and he knew it and wanted it even more than I did. On the eleventh day after his sister's wedding, in my kitchen, he told me he was in love with me and three weeks after that we had a big conversation in the Public Garden in Boston and he said that Octavia was a name he always loved if we ever had a girl. I had always thought that Octavia was one of the great names. There was no way in the world I could have escaped this love. It devoured us both.

We met each other's friends and cooked together and started fighting almost immediately. Our first fight was in Maine during the long Columbus Day weekend. We got in a fight about the fact that he had four cats that he had collected in his first marriage—four cats. The fight started slowly, but got heated and scary fast. It shocked me to fight so passionately with someone other than my mother (who during one of our fights when I was a teenager took a pair of shoes out of her closet, gave me one, and instructed me to throw it as hard as I could at the wall, and she threw the other one) that it sort of turned me on, but on the other hand I was pretty frightened of how strong the feelings were from both of us. We knew we had to work it out, though, because we were so in love that one fight or one thousand was not going to stop us. Neither one of us was going to say, Hold on, this feels insane, let's throw in the towel! So we started making chicken curry.

"All I meant to say was that, well, doesn't it seem obvious that your marriage was failing and you guys just kept getting more and more cats? Hoping that each one would fix the problem?" I said, using my best shrink language. We measured cumin.

"It's useless to equate a cat, a living thing—all of whom are very real and meaningful to me, I should reiterate—to a Band-Aid, no matter how convenient it might be for you. The fact is I have four cats," he said, shredding chicken.

"But I can't live in a New York apartment with four cats! Nobody would. There are all sorts of clichés that only crazy, lonely people live with multiple cats. And I love animals so I don't want to come out of this looking like some sort of animal rejecter," I said, now crying over simmering stock.

"You aren't an animal rejecter, but you must look at the reality of my life," he said, chopping the coriander.

"I can live with two cats," I said, and handed him the pepper mill.

"Well, I have four." He peppered.

We didn't solve it then but by the time the rice was done and the Major Grey's chutney was on the table we had stopped the bad fighting and decided since we were not moving in together yet (we had just met), we would "shelve" it until later. We were made up. We called it "The Working It Out Curry." I really thought we were smart to be able to get through a fight and make dinner at the same time.

But I digress. Starting this story with the lining-the-bathroom-walls-with-family-photos event is really what I wanted to do. Five years after we re-met, we had ended up in Oberlin—in a big 1877, redbrick house we never could have afforded on the East Coast. It was our second year in Ohio. Before we bought the house on Elm Street we had lived for a year in a rented faculty house, but when we saw "Bricky," as we called it, we could not help but buy it and renovate it into our dream house. We spent all our money and took out a home-equity loan for William Morris wallpaper and a new water heater. I wish I had a picture because I'll never be able to write how great it was.

My favorite thing that I still miss was a window seat I had put in the kitchen. When my parents built a country house in Connecticut, the architect said to my mother that teenagers will never talk to you unless your back is facing them, so put a sitting place behind the stove. Then they can lounge the way teenagers do while you cook, and apparently all sorts of their deep, dark life secrets will come out because they are not making eye contact with you. My mother insists to this day that the architect was right because according to her, we would hang out, all leggy and intense, and blab away while she made shirred eggs. Remembering that, I designed a little window seat to the side of the stove, perfect for Wallace and James to slump on when they were teenagers and I was cooking our supper. When you sat on it you looked up at these really old, tall pines that hugged that side of the house.

We had been living there for a week. I was downstairs

unpacking endless serving dishes his mother had given us. Julia, Josiah's mother, is one of the all-time most generous women. She wants her children and those who love them to have anything they ever desire. If you say you *might* need a serving tray or two for your new house, you will undoubtedly get at least six, and they will come wrapped in six rolls of paper towels, and sheets and sheets of bubble wrap, all bound by so much packing tape it will take you a half hour to cut through. She is from the deep South, as beautiful as Grace Kelly and thorough beyond belief. If she hadn't ended up married to a man (Josiah's stepfather) who traveled a lot and required a wife to run the household, I am positive she would have headed up NASA or MIT. She is a whiz at math.

Wallace ran in and out of the front door and James played with a lemon in a cardboard box. Josiah was upstairs ripping into boxes, hauling books into the guest room, but when I heard the clacking around of picture frames and spinning of measuring tapes my interest perked up. Leaving young James alone in the box—something ill advised that one always ends up doing in a multifloored house—I climbed the terrifyingly steep staircase and peeked into the bathroom. Josiah was on the floor, surrounded by all of our life in frames. "I'm hanging these in here," he said. I was so amazed and touched that I just left the house with the boys on a made-up trip to Home Depot in the neighboring town, which I would surely get lost trying to find. I was wholly in love with my life: two healthy children, a brilliant, tall (my father is tall and my mother when describing someone she approves of mentions if he or she is tall) professor husband who was carefully placing the evidence of our happy family all over the bathroom walls so everyone could see. When I came back, there in the main upstairs bathroom, was a love letter to our family, and to me. Frame after frame of generations of us, our people, and the little ones we made. It was security and peace, and everything I had always wanted.

Josiah left me and the boys a month later for a new member of the faculty. A female professor in his department hired to teach eighteenth-century English literature.

2

I am not a writer but I have been told I write good emails, which has led me to sit here at the library and tell this story. My story about me and Josiah is mine. Josiah could tell another view of the story and of course it would be different, but the end result for both of us is that we did get married and have children, and then we got divorced. The divorce part all happened in six months—although getting through a divorce when you have children actually takes a lifetime. The surviving it became my life rope. Turning the shirt right side in again started to define me and energize me. How I navigated it might just be my greatest accomplishment, like my own little *Sgt. Pepper's Lonely Hearts Club Band.* Going ahead in the story for a second, I remember my father coming into my childhood room in our New York apartment, where I had to return to from Ohio with my two boys after Josiah left. The room that once had Ranger Rick stickers on the mirror and posters of Duran Duran on the walls had been converted into my mother's office. I was sitting at the desk she had designed for herself, filling out a financial-aid application for a way-too-expensive nursery school that by a miracle I had gotten Wallace into midyear.

Daddy looked over my shoulder, put his hand on my head, and said, "Wanna hear something famous that Adlai Stevenson once said about Eleanor Roosevelt at her funeral?"

"Yeah," I said.

He said she was the kind of person who would rather light a candle than curse the darkness.

It has become my motto.

Soon after I married Josiah and after our first son Wallace was born we decided to follow his dream of being a professor over mine of being an actress. I was a working actress but was not famous or anything. At the beginning of my career, I had been in a smart independent movie, *Metropolitan,* that became kind of a WASP cult film. I had been on a few TV shows and in one very long-running, lucrative Luvs diaper commercial. Academic life seemed like a better life choice. It was steady, not much money, but lots of perks. Long summers, weird child-friendly hours in interesting college towns where you can live in rambling old houses with rosebushes tangled in the front yard for not much money. We would always be surrounded by youth and smart people, and I was versatile and friendly enough to make friends and a life pretty much wherever the academic job market winds blew us.

One thing I never knew until I married an academic was that getting a teaching job at a college is harder than being elected president, as far as I can see—and this is coming from an actress. It's a barbaric process that thousands of hardworking, *way* overly educated people slog through year after year, dearly hoping to get paid $43,000 at the University of Shagoog in North Who-knows-where Nevada. The process of narrowing down candidates takes six months. First, you scour through a list that comes out on October 15 of all the possible jobs open in your field nationally. Then, of course, because it is school we are talking about here, there's a series of tests that you must pass.

In Cambridge, where Josiah was adjunct teaching at Harvard, we lived in a crappy brown house that was nice enough from the outside, but inside smelled like dead animal. I think the entire place was floored in linoleum, and there was one shallow pink tub in a light brown tiled bathroom. The house also was like a walk-in refrigerator it was so cold. Never in my life have I been as cold as I was in Cambridge.

I was pregnant with James and taking a bath in that shallow tub when Josiah came in with a printed-out list and a map of the United States. He sat down on the little stool Wallace used to reach the sink to brush his teeth.

"Here's what we got. A twentieth-century English lit job at McGill, which I'll never get because I'm not Canadian. You know where McGill is?" he said, holding out the map. Ever since I went to my friend Vanessa's wedding in Montreal, I have always wanted to live there. I love French things, and in Montreal everything seems French. You can easily find a good baguette and it's a pretty drive to New York. Whenever I heard of any of these jobs I couldn't stop my mind from having us already living there—sort of like when you have a hot first date with someone, then later that night in your own bed you imagine your wedding. Montreal was a good fantasy.

"Won't they actually *like* it that you're not from Canada? Diversity?" I said.

"I wish. No, it's like a law there." He rechecked the list and sighed. "But then there is one at the University of Louisiana," he continued. I immediately thought too many snakes and no fresh vegetables.

"One at Fordham University." New York! "One at Harvard that I'll never get because it's really not a poetry job and I know the guy they want. But I might try," he says. Fine, it's Harvard . . . but I really can't stand Cambridge with all its frumpy pilgrims and sancti-mommies.

"And then there is an interesting one at Oberlin College in Ohio—I'm sort of scared to show you where it is on the map."

I held out a wet hand to take a good look. There was something in my gut (besides James) that made me know we were going to end up there. As I looked and the bathwater rolled over the Great Lakes and into the Midwest, he said, "It's sort of in the middle of nowhere, well, there's Cleveland, but I don't know that that's saying much. It's supposed to look like Connecticut, not that people from Connecticut believe that—does it make you want to scream?" he said.

"No, it doesn't," I said bravely. "It's supposed to be cool there, and fuck it, I bet we can get a house for two dollars."

So you apply. If you pass the first round of applications you submit a writing sample—hopefully part of a book that is about to be published (another impossible academic hoop to jump through), even though only three people will ever read it. Then you anxiously await a phone call made sometime in late December (ruining any holiday you might want to celebrate and, in our case, your son Wallace's birthday) inviting you to interview at a huge yearly conference where every university and college looking for a hire meets with all the academic hopefuls. It's called the Modern Language Association—or the MLA. If that goes well you may be asked to come give a talk (like teaching a class) at the actual college. This is the Wimbledon of getting a teaching job and it's exciting because you uncontrollably imagine you and your family plunked down in the middle of that beautiful college in the Berkshires, but that is dangerous because there are probably three to five candidates left in consideration. Then it's all a matter of praying that they won't notice you are not an Asian, lesbian, Jewish, black woman from Tanzania who did her undergraduate work at Yale and her grad work at Oxford—which is what all colleges and universities are dying to have on their staff. Hateful to say but true. When I was at college, if I'd had any idea how hard my teachers had to work to get the job, I would have done more of my reading.

Josiah ended up getting the Oberlin job. It was the first poetry job to come on the market in four years.

3

I had completely accepted the fact that I was going to take on the new role of housewife. A "stay-at-home mom" is a glamorous title that mothers in New York tend to use, but in the rest of the country where people rarely have nannies, Fresh Direct, or housekeepers, the more applicable term is housewife. I got a thrill out of knowing I was going to take on my children without help, cook every meal, and go it on my own in a new town where I knew nobody. I left a job on the television show *Law & Order: Special Victims Unit* playing the wife of the lead detective. A solid little job I had gotten when I was engaged to Josiah and we were both living in New York while he was writing his dissertation. Every once in a while they would fly me back to do a scene or two, but when I left New York I had really left acting and it had left me.

My mother had worked outside the house ever since I was three weeks old. For most of my life she ran a famous and powerful foundation in New York. She liked working hard and she was successful. Both of my parents were.

Now that I think of it, they always ran whatever it was they did. They were always the presidents or directors. Other kids' moms picked them up from school or were around at the playdates afterward, but if I wanted to see my mother during the day I went to her office on Park Avenue. Now that I know what the offices of other important people look like, I am endlessly impressed with how big and cool my mother's office was. She had a secretary named Marian who did lovely dictation and knew everything about where my mother was at all times in case my brother or I needed her.

The incredible thing about my mother, though, was that she would come home at six every night and cook supper for our family, which we ate together at the dining room table. I can remember hearing the door open and she would call, "Cooo cooo!" then the door would slam and she would go directly into the kitchen to unload the pork chops or fish that she had bought on the way home from work.

"We have the cod cakes from Rosedale's on the East Side toniiiight!" she would call.

I think she thought food from the East Side was better than food from the West Side, where we lived. The fact that my mother worked so hard never got in the way of her being a marvelous cook, hostess, and homemaker. She never was late with a permission slip, I always had a clean purple shirt for "purple shirt day" at school, and there was always a bunch of fresh flowers next to her armchair in the living room and Mallomars in the cupboard. I never heard her say she was tired or complain one bit about having to make dinner or sew ribbons on toe shoes. If we got sick she made us get out of bed while she remade it. "Nothing is worse than a falling-apart bed when you are sick," she would say as she beat the daylights out of the sheets. I don't know how she did it, and let me tell you, living up to her example hasn't been easy.

The first time I ever saw Ohio was when Wallace, James, a summer babysitter, and I arrived to meet Josiah, who had gone out ahead of us to set up shop. We had flown from Maine, where we had all just spent the summer. One mom, one two-year-old, one three-month-old nursing baby, and one shy, blond Dutch Reformed babysitter from deep in the woods of Canada. My father (always ready to give you a ride) drove us two hours to the airport. Then the plan was to take two planes, one from Portland to Newark and one from there to Cleveland to meet Josiah. My father, as he left us at the gate in Portland, looked like someone sending four toddlers into Penn Station. Like parachuters, Molly (the babysitter) and I had purses and diaper bags strapped all over us. We each had a kid, snacks, picture books under our arms, and our hair stuffed in ponytails. I was trying to be organized, but the first thing that happened was that a kind (thank God) security guard noticed that my driver's license was expired by *six months*. By a miracle she let us on the plane anyway (remember Portland was the airport the 9/11 bombers sailed through three years before) and somehow we arrived in Cleveland, where Josiah was waiting for us. When we had finally piled in the minivan that he had driven out to Ohio, I asked him before we left the terminal what was for supper.

"I don't know—I have been at Sears all day in Elyria buying a washing machine," he said.

Even though I had a faint idea that spending the day in Elyria, Ohio, at Sears buying a washing machine was probably a taxing endeavor, the fact that he had not managed to come up with a plan for our first night together in what was sure to be the next huge chapter in our life made me feel like he had ripped off my wedding ring, flung it on the road, and told us all to walk to Oberlin.

"Are you kidding?" I said, the tears welling up.

"Are *you*?" he said.

For the next twenty minutes I sat in the front seat with my head pressed on the rolled-up window, quietly sobbing. Outside, I could see the enormous, looming industrial (and famously empty) factories from the turn of the century, and miles and miles of suburban strip-mall sprawl that you see in most of the country.

I cried for my life in New York and for my parents, whom I had just left in Maine, and for my broken dream that I had married a man who would have a dinner plan for his family who had just given up everything to join him. I cried because my New York license had expired and the next one I'd get would be an Ohio license. I cried for my children having to say they were from the Midwest. I cried because it was spoiled to cry. I cried and cried and cried. Josiah had ruined our first day there for me and I had ruined it for him by not saying thank you for dealing with the washing machine and by crying for half an hour on the drive to our new little town. He tried to give me a tour of the various school buildings and point out the IGA supermarket, but I was in my own world of misery. We just missed that chance one has for a good shared experience and ended up having our own solitary bad ones. We constantly did that to each other—we wouldn't plan well enough not to have a fight at an important time.

Now that I think about it, we had a fight maybe at every important time. Wallace's christening was ruined because the godfather, Josiah's best friend, had flown in from his teaching job at Iowa to celebrate with us. He and Josiah went out way too late and drank way too much. I was livid by the time they got home and ranted deep into the night about how Josiah had let me down instead of getting a good sleep. If we had had any foresight, we could have avoided it altogether. Of course they were going to go out and have fun, but of course I couldn't be blamed for wanting a not-hungover husband on the first day of my son's life as a Christian. We botched that day. We botched a lot of days. If I had ever been able to let go of my jealousy about ex-girlfriends, or if he had let go of ex-girlfriends, we could have avoided hours of fighting and replaced them with nicer times, but we couldn't. We often couldn't see the other person's way. So we fought. And we were fighting now on the eve of our new life together.

It was our gray faculty house that saved the day. It was worn from years of professors and their families making their lives for a bit of time in it. It was like a bird's nest that just stays in the tree for years while different birds use it to raise their young. It was warm, generous, and smelled of must and wood. There was an enormous lilac bush in the yard that I knew in the spring would bring me endless happiness, as I would be able to fill the house over and over again with the light and dark purple, intensely fragrant flowers that blossomed three weeks a year. It was a jolly house and it saved our night and possibly the first year of our lives in Oberlin. The second I stepped into the double living room with the dark beams on the ceiling and the beautifully paned windows all around, I knew we would be happy there. We put the kids to sleep in their new rooms. I took a bath upstairs and Josiah went out for Chinese food and bought a bottle of wine for me. Molly, the babysitter, Josiah, and I sat on boxes, ate shrimp and broccoli, and toasted our safe arrival and our new lives.

4

Molly left the next day to go teach preschool in Michigan, and Josiah went to the English department to settle in. I was left to organize and settle the boys and get myself acquainted with the house and town. There were bumps and moments of sheer panic, like when I failed my Ohio driver's license test by knocking into three cones when I was trying to parallel park our minivan. In New York you take your driver's license test on Delancey Street in Lower Manhattan with all the traffic and pedestrians swarming around, so I thought an empty parking lot would be a cinch, but no. Also, for three entire days I honestly believed that there was no cable television in Ohio. But quite soon, like a week in, I got the overwhelming sense that the world was mine to have if I wanted it. Life felt good right away. Oberlin feels like fertile ground. Like if you have a plan or an idea, you can make it happen there. I felt like a pioneer. I knew when a place was not going to work. I had had that feeling in Cambridge, and this felt entirely different and exciting.

During that first year there were two things that really turned me on. One was a little organic farm just outside of town and one was the 2004 presidential election. Oberlin the city was established in 1833, at the same time as Oberlin the college. It was the very first college in the country to accept everyone—women, men, any race or religion—right from the very start. Because the college is the town and the town is the college, it's a very liberal place to live. This was perfect for Josiah and me, two overeducated lefties just like our parents before us. We reveled in the fact that our faculty house was right next to the environmental building where they recycled poo-poo (they actually had a program where they paid you twenty-five cents to use their facilities—it was called the Poo-Poo Project) and across the lane from the only nudist dorm in America. The very first weekend we got there we went to a tiny (really I cannot impress upon you enough how tiny everything is) farmers' market. At the biggest stand there was a girl farmer in a backward baseball hat. She had dirt all over her jeans and a Hershey's bar T-shirt that looked great because of her Susan Sarandon–like bosom. She grabbed handfuls of beans and beets like a jewel merchant in Burma. I had James in the BabyBjörn and Wallace was running around dancing to the drumming of three students with their djembes. Whenever I picture Oberlin there is always some eighteen-year-old scruffy student playing a didgeridoo in the background. This setting was perfect for Wallace. He came out of the womb with an unusual and amazing sensitivity to music. When he was only three months old, and Josiah would sing one of his standard lullabies, "All Night, All Day," my little baby would swell with real emotion. His eyes rimmed with tears and his face crumbled into a million pieces. It got so we couldn't sing the song to him because it was just too heartbreaking.

Going along with the housewife plan to cook every meal, I bought armfuls of zucchini and tomatoes from the girl farmer. As I was shelling out barely seven dollars for thirty pounds of vegetables, my New York opportunistic mind got to thinking, How can I use this scene to my advantage? I listened to the crowds. "Lydia, are the squash ready this week?" "Lydia, will you have turkeys this year?" "Lydia, where are the duck eggs?"

"Umm, Lydia . . . ?" I piped in as if I was one of the regulars. "Can I bring my kids to your farm to help you pick tomatoes?" I pronounce *tomato* like my mother does, with an *ah* sound (tom*ah*to) instead of a long *a* sound (tom*a*to). It's very Anglophilic and it irked Josiah.

Without missing a beat she glanced at Wallace dancing with abandon under the apple tree and with a slight lisp, because of the piercing in her tongue, said, "Hell, yes."

We spent the next three months tromping through the thick, weedy, lush grass that grows wild in between the tomato vines. We picked green zebras, heirloom golds, red Italian-looking ones, and the light orange baby ones that taste better than candy. Sometimes I would look down at Wallace, who had squatted to catch a grasshopper or roll a rock, and he was a chipmunk. His cheeks filled with the juicy pulp—seeds and tomato water all over his shirt. My little New York–born child was growing up on an organic farm! I believed that through osmosis he was turning into someone who would care about the earth and hard work and good people who knew when the sun rose and set. I would imagine my friends hauling their strollers around that dirty city from one $500 music class to another and I would feel so lucky that fate had handed me another option.

Lydia the farmer, who was twenty-three and surprisingly flighty for a farmer, grew and harvested the vegetables with one willowy assistant named Lillian, who went to the college. She would sell her loot to Dan, her boyfriend, who owned the only fantastic lunch place in town, Black River. All the college kids and professors ate there almost every day. There is a place like this in every college town (*Gourmet* should do a story on them)—good soups, muffins, omelets, and really strong coffee that you bring your own mug for. Dan was thirty with salt-and-pepper hair in a ponytail, tall with nice brown eyes and a big Roman nose. The two of them looked like people Herb Ritts would've liked to have photographed, and together created the best BLT I have ever eaten. They both had gone to Oberlin, but at different times, and they did that laid-back activist thing that Oberlin students are so good at. At the end of the cycle Dan would give Lydia the leftovers from the college kids' plates, which she would feed to the pigs. It was a romantic partnership and so sexy because they were proud of each other. They needed each other as a couple and for their business. Romantic sustainable agriculture. I loved it. They were also both really nice to my kids.

And it was movie-set beautiful, too. The farm was overtaken with flowers. They lined the dirt roads and peppered the fields. There were planted flowers, like sunflowers and lilies, and there were also masses of wild

Queen Anne's lace and goldenrod, the stuff that makes everyone sneeze, but looks pretty in bouquets. I know about flowers because of my mother and her gardens. My mother has always had a garden. Both her grandmothers, Josephine and Hope, had gardens. I am very sure that one definition my mother has for a real lady, one of the highest compliments she gives, is that she has or loves a garden. On the kitchen table in Maine there is always a small vase (pronounced with a hard *a* instead of an *ah*) of yellow, orange, and red nasturtiums. Or if we are lucky with the weather that year, bunches of viny, aromatic sweet peas. She loves marigolds because they are sturdy and bright, but dislikes their smell. Mum pronounces the Greek names of the flowers proudly and gets cross with herself if she forgets one. Anyway, a love of flowers is one of the things my mother passed down to me that did not go in the garbage. The farm I was spending all my time at was run wild with them.

"I just can't deal with the fucking flowuhs," Lydia said in her really thick Boston accent. "The fahmah beforh me went crazy with 'em and I don't know shit about 'em or what to do with 'em."

It was Josiah who came up with the Ball jar idea. I would pick the flowers, arrange them in canning jars, and sell them at the farmers' market for ten bucks each. There were twelve 16-ounce Ball jars that came in a flat at the hardware store (one of the seven stores in Oberlin), so if I sold them all, Lydia would make $120. Big stuff for a small-stuff organic farmer. I would get the pleasure and satisfaction of "working" at the farm and participating in the community. So we did it. On Fridays I would drive just outside of town to the farm after Josiah got home from the office. He got home at six each night even though he only taught for about forty-five minutes three times a day. But apparently there was lots of *grading* (the bane of all teachers) to be done and book writing and student office hours. For a profession where one can be at home 50 percent of the time, Josiah sure stuck to that six o'clock hour. But even at six, at least for the early fall, I still had two hours until the sun set to pick and arrange. I ran up and down the dirt road and darted in and out of the rows in special farm boots I had bought at the Army Navy store, with my big kitchen scissors and a basket, cutting cutting cutting every flower in sight. I had rigged a random door I found in the barn to crates where I would set up the Ball jars. Then I filled each one with extraordinarily cold water from the hose on the side of the barn. There was no electricity at the farm, so if the sun set too fast (or I was too slow), I'd turn on the headlights of the Honda Odyssey and arrange the flowers in the beams, looking like Babe Paley, the famous hostess. It was fun. By the time I had loaded up my minivan with the arrangements that would stay in the back until I brought them early the next morning to the market to be sold, Josiah had gotten the boys to sleep and would be waiting for me in our rented faculty house with a bowl of nut pesto spaghetti and a glass of wine. I didn't think it could get much better than that.

5

The flowers turned out to be quite a hit. People who live in small college towns are usually very sophisticated, overeducated, and culture starved. They have a little more money to spend because they live in Ohio instead of New York or Boston, where lots of them are from, so blowing ten dollars for a jar of fresh-cut flowers is something they are chomping at the bit to do. I became a little more known to the community as well. It was too cute and intriguing to see the brand-new faculty wife with her two towheaded boys selling flowers on Saturday morning at a farmers' market in *Ohio*. You might think I am being delusional about the amount of interest that was taken in me and my family, but in all honesty, there are only a few new families or faculty members that come to the tiny spaceship in the middle of farmland each year, and people, including myself, are as curious and nosey as the Stepford wives in Darien about who is who. In fact, coming from New York, where you could be living next to Pavarotti and not know it or particularly care, in Ohio you live in a fishbowl, and once you are swimming in the bowl, your life might as well be everyone's business.

The flowers did eventually die in the fields and the snow began to fall. Starting in the late fall and all through the winter into spring, it snows constantly in Oberlin. It's called lake-effect snow. There is some pressure system that hovers over the Great Lakes, causing very light, gentle snow to fall pretty much every day. When I imagined the Midwest, and Ohio in particular, I thought it would be flat and boring. But because of those lakes causing all that weather, there are extremely dramatic low-cloud formations. At many times of day you can see what people call "God light." It's when the sun streams through thick clouds and it looks like God is beaming a message down or performing a miracle on someone who lives in a neighboring town. I think because I was defensive about moving away from New York, I was always looking for reasons why our life was just as good as the lives of the friends I had left behind. The extreme beauty of the weather was something I comforted myself with—all those tall buildings in New York block the sky, and I got huge, Technicolor canvases of majestic weather beauty all day long. The drama of the weather was also a great backdrop to the drama that was about to unfold in our lives, but not quite yet, so when you are reading later, just remember the clouds and snow.

On the farm, when the winter creeps in and the first frost happens, the basil turns black. It's ugly and you can't believe that in one day rows and rows of vibrant, green, great-smelling basil can all just suddenly go black and dead. This transition marked the end of the farm for me.

Not because I wanted it to end, but because Lydia broke up with Dan and decided to go to vet school. So she ditched the farm. I was so disappointed in her. I thought farmers were true to their word and the land, standing by the frozen ground! I had dreams of becoming the next Midwestern Ina Garten. I was going to take the organic flowers nationwide and put our little farm on the map—like Diane Keaton did in *Baby Boom* with the applesauce. But it didn't happen because my would-be partner Lydia didn't want to stay the course, and as I soon learned better than I ever wanted to, when one person really wants to go there is nothing you can do about it but watch them.

During those starting-off months I saw our family life in two parts: Josiah doing his job at the college, and me and the kids showing him that we were okay—thriving, in fact. I wanted him to be proud of me. I wanted him to brag to his mother about what a good sport I was, that within a week I was practically starting a business at a farm. I am an approval seeker. For as long as I can remember I have always wanted the approval of some mother figure. Lots of people doubted that I would be all right out there, but I was all right and I wanted big credit for it. Did Josiah feel pressure about my happiness? Maybe, but why shouldn't he feel some responsibility for taking me and the kids way out there? Nobody put a gun to my head. I had encouraged him to teach—he is so good at it. We had spent our first years struggling to make life work together and I was going to prove to everyone, including myself, that it did. After all, we had two babies and moved five times in three years. Would anyone blame us for some hard times? Some difficulty? A few whopper fights? I had been cranky, but I had been pregnant and nursing. When I am pregnant my niceness goes down 40 percent. So perhaps I had not been at the top of my game. On the other side, if I had been 40 percent less nice during those two years, he had been 40 percent more remote and hard to reach. *But* he was trying to get a job and publish a book. We were feeling the burn, and frankly, I was proud that we were making it, even if we did fight badly sometimes. We didn't just stay in our cushy, too expensive New York life with our friends, we went out like Ernest Shackleton on the *Endurance* and forged new territory. I was proud of us. I saw us as a team and also what I had signed up for. If I had to move to the Sahara I would have, because I was married and because I was in love with him.

And a lot of our life was blissful, at least for me. Like Maine. Like swimming off the dock in Maine. Because Josiah taught school, we could spend long summers in my favorite place on earth. What's nice about academic life is that you revert back to the school-year calendar. September to May and then the summer. One of the major reasons we picked his academic career over my acting career is that our families still had houses on the island in Maine where we spent every summer growing up. My mother's family has had the house there for generations. I could get into a whole Maine thing and spend the rest of this book describing the rocky coastlines and the summer island communities and all the WASPyness, but I won't because lots of other people do that and it's not the point of the story. But it is a place that defines me in lots of ways.

My kids are the sixth generation to live in this house during the summer. It started way back in the late 1800s with a woman named Anna. She married a wealthy Philadelphia banker who helped found the summer community. Anna was a beauty. I know because I have seen a picture of a portrait of her painted by John Singer Sargent. (Of course no one has a clue where that God-knows-how-much-it-would-be-worth painting is now.) From her, the house was passed down and down and down a ladder of women. Some loved it, some didn't. Some decades it was abandoned, some it was filled to capacity, but my mother ended up with it. My brothers and I have romped around the place for all the summers of our lives.

It's a matriarchy up there, and frankly, the men don't really count. Oh, they are around—you see them sailing in their Irish fishing sweaters on the weekends and driving in their jalopies to the one market on the island. (WASPs don't drive expensive, fancy cars in the summer. In fact, you can't tell at all if they have money or not until you arrive for dinner at their sixteen-bedroom cottage on the sea that they only occupy for the summer months.) Traditionally, the women would bring the children up for the summer to get them away from the hot, tubercular northeastern cities, and the men would stay to be at the office. This meant the women ruled the houses, the club, the staff, the children, and the social order. Nothing has changed since 1900. All the women in my family, including my mother, were grandes dames. Powerhouse women in their own little worlds. Lots of expectations about how things should be done and *lots* of opinions about how things should not be done. Always arrive for a dinner at someone's house with a little bouquet of flowers from your own garden, or the side of the road if you don't have a garden. Never talk about business on the porch at the yacht club. Never complain about the weather unless there has been too little rain and the garden is parched. Always give some amount of money to all the charities on the island. I have bought into the whole thing. When I am up there I run the junior activities committee, have lots of dinner parties, play tennis with the children and then without the children while some aimless teenager takes them to the beach to look for crabs. It works perfectly if you have the summer off guilt-free because your husband teaches college. Josiah had proposed to me on our dock in Maine. We conceived James in Maine. He had also been baptized in Maine. We had our honeymoon in Maine. We spent our summers together in Maine. We even spent six months into the winter while Josiah finished his dissertation up in Maine, so our son Wallace learned to walk there. And because we knew each other as children in Maine, we would be forever entwined in it and its rocky beaches and summer cottages.

Josiah used to tell the story that as a young boy he had a fantasy I would fall off the yacht club dock and he would jump into the water to save me. As a young girl, I never even thought about Josiah, mostly because my friend Polly had such a crush on him. I remember seeing him at dances or on the dock and the only thing I felt was intimidated by him (he was a year older than me), so later when I learned that I had it wrong, that he wanted to be my hero, it was endlessly romantic to me. The truth is, on that foggy night at his sister's wedding, I did feel he was my hero.

Josiah used to be the only dad there during the week

until all the other dads flew up (usually from their banking jobs) on Friday. I think it drove him crazy and chopped his dick off a bit. He would write during the day, which meant he didn't have to sit around the yacht club at lunch with the masses of children, au pairs, and mothers still in their tennis clothes with a Ralph Lauren cable-knit sweater thrown on top. Josiah completely looked the part. But he wasn't. Josiah could get dark. Thinking about it now, I realize he is truly a mystery. He is southern and well mannered. His southern mother, Julia, a beauty queen, who once held the title Maid of Cotton, made sure all four of her children knew how to get along in any company they were to keep. All those kids are very congenial. Josiah went to Groton, Yale, Johns Hopkins, and Harvard. He is no slouch. He is well-spoken but has a very quiet voice. He is vastly interested in what the other person is doing and thinking, but reveals almost nothing about himself, so you can go through an entire friendship, even a marriage, with him and not know what *he* is thinking and doing.

We had a million nicknames for each other, many of them deriving from animals. We ended up with the somewhat silly but normal, as those things go, nickname "Bully." We played characters and had voices that we used. It felt very intimate and loving. Secret languages and characters. When Josiah toasted me at our wedding, he toasted my imagination. I wept as he unveiled for all our friends and family what it was like to live with my interior life. I thought it was so unusual of him to toast my insides instead of my surface, what I looked like on the way to a cocktail party or the way I was on a daily basis. In retrospect I'm not really sure he liked who I was on a daily basis, or maybe he was bored by it, or didn't relate to it, or worst of all looked down on it. I made him listen to Céline Dion instead of Mozart. We watched *Survivor* and played Celebrity with our friends after dinner. Some of his friends from the past marveled at how he had changed from being such a complicated, intellectual eccentric to this out-in-the-open husband of a blond New York actress who spent his summers in Maine. I just thought I had seen a hidden part of him that he liked and wanted to be, and was giving him a life where he could be a happy, lighthearted family man who liked a party as much as the rest.

He would sometimes do funny things that felt exactly like me. One time right at the start of our relationship we had gone out for a really big boozy night with his grad school pals. I was so hungover and hungry the next morning, I couldn't bear the thought of removing myself from the bottom of the bed. So Josiah went out and came back with a gigantic bag from McDonald's and *The New York Times.* "I thought Mickey D's would serve us well this morning"—it was around noon—"but I didn't know what you would like, so I got you everything—even the Filet-O-Fish sandwich." I laughed for a half hour. I thought we were the same, or told myself we were.

I wish I had this poem of his that he read me right at the start of our romance. We were lying in bed, probably naked, in his room in Cambridge.

"Read me one of your poems," I said.

"I could. Lots are unfinished," he said.

"I don't care, but I don't want to hear one about Samantha or Edith."

I was insecure about the women in his past. They too, like Josiah, had been smart, complex, odd birds. They had dark hair and tiny frames. I felt like a huge yellow stork compared to them. Like Carol Burnett to their Isabelle Adjani.

"No, no," he said in an understanding way so I didn't feel bad about being so fucking insecure.

He pulled one out of one of the six thousand manila folders he had in his files and started reading. His speaking voice, although quiet, is very deep. Very deep. He really should do voice-overs. He reads poetry the way all poets do. There is a lilting rhythm to it. All of them have it—it's like how all newscasters sound the same. It comes with the trade. So there we are in his room and he starts reading and what unfolds from his mouth is the darkest, scariest, most raw poem I have ever heard. It's like if Joe Strummer, Edgar Allan Poe, and Sylvia Plath had a baby and it wrote a poem.

"My God," I barely said.

"Yeah," he said, and put the poem away. "I wrote that during all of that complicated time with Samantha."

Man, it was dark. And truthfully I had no idea what it meant. I just thought that maybe I was too dumb to get it and he was so brilliant and in touch with his way deep deep feelings that I just shouldn't say anything. So I didn't—ever again. I think it hurt his feelings and he might have felt embarrassed by my lack of response, or maybe he just thought I was dim. He never read me another poem for the next six years and I know he wrote a lot of them. Again, we ignored warning signs. Was it just love? Love must be extraordinarily powerful for so many people to ignore dangerous, red, blaring warning signs—or not to be able to see them at *all* until it is too late. How do you see them? If you have the ability to really open yourself to love and dig down in it, maybe you are in for some trouble if you are not lucky enough to pick the right person. Is it random? I think you just have to make these great big mistakes to learn. And then I think the key is to think hard about what you want to have and want to avoid before you fall in love again. Once you are in love I don't think you have a lot of choices. You just have to ride it out. That's it. Love gives you no choices.

But we were so close. That first year in Oberlin, we would go on these long walks around the campus, with the boys in a double stroller. Josiah would make tea in Ball jars to bring along. If we saw anyone at all, I could feel them looking at us and marveling at how lovely it all seemed. I too felt it was a perfect picture and felt lucky that it was mine. We would come home, put the boys to sleep for an afternoon nap, and retire to our room as well. There were these foggy, misty days—not rain, but mist and wet. If it was cold enough the mist would freeze on the bare trees and the entire world looked like Narnia. Josiah and I would get in bed, make love, and talk about what houses were for sale in town.

"We can't buy the one on Maple, it had nine bedrooms, I think it may have been a bed-and-breakfast," I would say.

"But why else do we live in Ohio if not to have nine bedrooms? Maybe we can have nine children! And it's pink," he said.

"Okay, let's have nine children and I'll also run a pink bed-and-breakfast."

"Okay, my love."

"I hate bed-and-breakfasts."

"So do I."

Then we would read the paper and fall asleep. And that could all happen on a Wednesday.

6

Our first year went on like that. We were fine. We were steadily making more and more friends, we found charming country places where our boys could play, and there was the presidential election of 2004. I took that on like the flowers. Northeast Ohio was a political hotbed. It was purple on all the CNN maps because its citizens did not know who to vote for. People came from the East to live there and work for their candidate just to try and sway these important voters to either side. It was really exciting. I volunteered in the tiny Democratic office in town. It took up one room in the only hotel in town, but it had six phone lines, and six people would cram in there every night of October and work the phone bank. I went every other night from 6 to 9 p.m. The election took over everyone's lives. I felt like I was working in John Kerry's headquarters. The baby and Wallace wore Kerry buttons. It was all I thought about and really all Josiah and I talked about. My New York friends envied me because if you were in Ohio you could help make a difference. Bush was evil and needed to get out of office, and our entire world was motivated to make sure he did. It ended on the rainiest Election Day I will ever see. The night before, the weatherman warned of heavy, nonstop rains for the following day all across the Midwest. Josiah and I waited in line for six hours each to vote, so twelve hours in total. On election night the last state to turn red was Ohio and Kerry lost. During his concession speech the next day I sat on our sofa and cried as if my mother had died.

Josiah was thriving in his department and loving the teaching. He had been teaching at Harvard the year before, but even though the kids were off-the-charts smart they didn't have the élan, style, curiosity, creativity, and bravado that the Oberlin students have. Oberlin students are named Zack or Violet. They know transgendered people and how to address them, never making a mistake. I am forever getting confused on that account. Sometimes it's very hard to tell what gender these kids are, and I suppose that is the point. There was one person who worked at the bookstore. The person's name was Terry. Like I said, I couldn't tell. I believed he was originally a boy, but was gender identified as being a lesbian girl and was on his/her way physically to actually being a girl. I figured that out because he/she wore a button that said "Lesbian Bitch." Terry was very sweet and helpful at the bookstore but there was also nothing about his/her body that would be recognized as either sex. I really tried, but always felt nervous and uncool around this person. Nobody else seemed to have a problem dealing with him/her as far as I could see. Oberlin students usually play an instrument well, even if they are not in the world-renowned conservatory that is also part of the school. The most noticeable characteristic, though, is that they always think they are right. I know this because during the spring semester of our first year I got a job teaching acting for the camera to seniors for the following fall. It's hard to get a job teaching college anywhere, but I got lucky thanks to George. (And being on *Law & Order* didn't hurt.)

George, a senior member of the theater department, actually lived next door to us with his partner, Paul, who worked in a science lab at the college, so they didn't have to look that hard for me. George and Paul were heaven to live next door to because they were the perfect Martha Stewart–loving gay couple. They looked great, cooked beautifully, entertained, gardened, and had two adorable cockadoodles that the boys loved to play with. If you needed fresh thyme for a recipe they would have it in their garden next to the sage and chives ("that have absolutely gone ballistic!" they would say), and they'd urge you to take a bunch of that too and toss it in the salad. They felt trapped being in rural Ohio, where the quickest way to get someone to vote Republican is by threatening a law allowing gay marriage, but also felt safe because of the liberal nature of our town. And they knew they were appreciated by lost foodies like Josiah and me who oohed and aahed over the horseradish dressing they served with the beef. So when they had us over and asked if I would apply for the adjunct teaching position in the theater department, I felt like I had won the lottery.

Now we were really set up. In the fall, I would have something meaningful to do that was finally in Josiah's world. People would say, "Oh, that's Josiah Robinson, the poetry professor, and his wife, Isabel, who teaches in the theater department." Josiah was proud and excited . . . I think. If there was any territorial jealousy I didn't notice, or I chose to ignore it. I still was safe in my TV-land box and he could be the big daddy intellectual securely fastened in the highly respected English department.

Late that spring we stumbled across a redbrick house set back from the road with two enormous maple trees in the front yard. It was a little expensive compared to what else was out there, but it was gorgeous, and my friends in New York were paying six times as much for boxes that looked at brick walls, so I felt very house proud. As the students dribbled out of town for the summer, I spent all my time tearing pages out of *House & Garden* and begging New York fabric houses to send samples to Ohio. We ripped out the kitchen and designed a new one. We covered the walls in the William Morris wallpaper and left for Maine like victorious soldiers coming home from the war.

There was one other thing that happened that spring. As a member of the English department, Josiah had to meet with all of the candidates who were hoping to land a job at Oberlin for the following year. There was an eighteenth-century English hire that had to be made. Not that I understand why, but this position had been very difficult to fill. They kept hiring people to teach it as adjuncts and simply could not find the right person to fill the tenure-track position. They did eventually land on this guy Robert who was to come from Princeton. But when he visited, he got turned off by the infinitesimal size and weirdness of everything. He also had a boyfriend on the East Coast. He ended up deferring the job for one year. So the department tossed the net back out again and pulled in another Princeton fish who had just completed her Ph.D. in eighteenth-century English. Her name was Sylvia Legard. As everyone hears everything about anybody who has come or even *might* come to town, I had heard about this young girl. My pal Rebecca had also gone to Princeton and knew her. Rebecca said she was pretty and was to be married that summer. She also said I would like her.

One day in late spring Josiah came home from work later than usual, maybe by twenty minutes. Wallace, James, and I were lolling around on the front lawn of our rented faculty house, playing with a hose and getting ready to grill for supper. We lived on a little cul-de-sac that only had faculty housing on it. There were five houses. One was us; the next George and Paul; then there was the athletic director, Mick (I was a tad surprised to find out that Oberlin actually had an athletic department), and his family, whom we never saw; a religion professor, Jane, and her husband and two girls our boys' age; and then a physics professor and his wife, a composer who was an adjunct composing professor at the conservatory. In the spring we would set up one grill in our yard and everyone would come over around six thirty with their various meats and veggies to grill. We would all flop on the grass and picnic until it got dark. This was one of those nights.

"Bully!" Josiah called as he swept a running Wallace up into his arms.

"Bully!" I echoed. I loved it when he came home. "You are home entirely too late, my love—we almost started without you," I said while kissing him. By this time Jane's girls were stomping around, playing with the hose as well.

"I know, I was interviewing. That eighteenth-century woman is here, Sylvia. I had to interrogate her," he said.

"Oh! What is she like? Will she get it? Will I like her?" I said while helping James step over the side of the curb. He was learning to walk.

"Well, I don't know that she's got it. Her talk was okay. Didn't blow me out of the water. But you will like her. She's French, sort of," he said, then grabbed James, who was naked, pressed his mouth on his tummy, and blew a lot of air out. It made a huge farting sound and James fell into hysterical laughter.

That was all we ever said about Sylvia that spring. She ended up getting the job.

7

I called the following summer in Maine "the summer of love." Obviously you never know when the bus is going to hit you, but I had always thought that if something as dramatic as your marriage ending was about to happen you would have some sense of it. There would be a tone change or a subtle undercurrent that you might feel—certainly that I would feel. But I missed any signs of trouble. There was one time that Josiah got particularly miffed at me for overcooking the crab. That made me pause, but he was so particular about everything in the kitchen, I didn't read anything into it.

I remember us swimming a lot in the ocean. It was really warm that summer (probably because of global warming), so everyone was constantly in the sea. One day while the kids napped, Josiah and I went down to the dock for a swim. (My mother was cooking. My mother is always cooking something. Her best dish is cheese soufflé. She sometimes gathers friends in a miniclass and teaches them how to make it. They learn how to cook the soufflé and then they all sit down to a proper lunch with red wine. But on that day she was baking chocolate chip cookies. "You two go have a swim," she ordered.)

Josiah swam laps back and forth from our dock to the Davises' sailboat. I sort of did laps, but more would just swim here and there, lying back to float and look up at the sky every so often. We met back on the dock and hung off the ladder, each of us holding on to a different side.

"Are we ever going to have a Labrador?" I said.

"Yes," he said.

"What color? I always imagined I'd have a black one, but maybe you don't like black?"

"Well, you just might be right about that. I might just think what we need are two yellow Labs. One for Wallace and one for James."

"Ohhh, yes. You are right. Two yellow Labs. What will their names be?" We loved to name things.

"Wallace and James," he said, and bubbled away, down to touch the bottom.

See? Summer of love. No big fighting, just slight irritation about cooking times and lots of talk about yellow Labs.

We all drove back to Oberlin at the end of August, across the Berkshires and over the mountains of New York state. Besides the excitement about my new house, what was on my mind was my new job.

It turns out that I love to teach. At first I ripped off my own teacher from New York. I assigned her books, used her syllabus to fashion my own, and, embarrassing as this is, I imitated her voice. Rose was a short, hotheaded Scottish firecracker. We were all terrified of her and worshiped her. She said things like, "Oh, this is bullshit. If you are going to phone shit like this in, do it on your own time—don't waste mine. If you have to act, then do it right, but if you can do anything else, then don't clutter the business." She was a hard-ass. She always looked great in class, too. She wore brown leather pants with high-heeled boots and cashmere yoke sweaters. She was only five feet tall, but she had the presence of Vanessa Redgrave, intimidating and attractive at the same time. So I was on the phone with her a lot asking for advice, and I summoned her spirit and regenerated it in my own little class on the bottom floor of the drama department. Somewhat surprisingly, I was a hard-ass too—I loved it.

I had always noticed when Josiah would go off to teach that there was a game face he put on. He was like an athlete going to the stadium. There were certain clothes that were teaching clothes and there were rituals. He had a cup of tea at his desk about twenty minutes before class. He got in the zone. Until I started teaching and became part of the faculty, I thought he was the only one who did that, but it seems that all professors have some version of Josiah's ritual. I felt like I was on a pro football team. If a friend said, "I'm about to teach," that was code for "We have to stop talking now so I can get in the zone." People looked better on teaching days. It feels exciting before you face the class, and there is a certain amount of energy and focus you must summon in order to step in front of a bunch of kids in their late adolescence and hope to raise awareness, enlighten, and convey information. I had a very particular routine:

I taught from 2 to 4 p.m. on Mondays, Wednesdays, and Fridays. Wallace, the three-year-old, was at day care during those hours, so I didn't have to worry about him. (Although I did because he hated day care. Even at three I think he felt misunderstood. He loves Cirque du Soleil where other kids like Thomas the Train. He asks what language people are speaking in delis and when he was two said things like "It's a mystery.") At noon, Grace, Josiah's star English student, would walk across our backyard, carrying the oversized pottery coffee cup that she had made herself, to take care of James.

"Hey, man," she would say as she took off her boots in the kitchen. "Where is the little guy?"

At that point fifteen-month-old James would toddle into the kitchen looking like a Cossack. "Hey, buddy!" she would say like the hippie kid she was. Then the two of them would twirl away on some little adventure before his lunch (Grace would sometimes bring him some chunky quinoa vegetable salad or a monstrous carrot muffin from her food co-op) and nap. I never worried about James when he was with Grace. I once saw them on the quad with a bunch of her friends. There was my James, the fifteen-month-old, in a sea of tie-dye and Hacky Sacks, living it up, a preview of what will surely come.

Once Grace had James, I would run upstairs and change into teaching clothes. You always want your students to think you look great and to be intimidated by you. It's tricky, the student/teacher relationship. You must be close enough so they feel they can open themselves to you and learn, but not so close that they think you are their friend and can ask you where you got your clothes. You are older than they are, cooler, have much more under your belt. There are times when you don't feel that way, but you must never let them know that. Never let them see you flustered or having a fight with your husband or buying tampons at the store. You must remain elusive, but at the same time you want them to want to know you, so you give little bits here and there. Delicate. When I was dressed and feeling good, I got my teaching bag and headed to lunch at Black River. There I would sit at the counter, have the soup of the day, and go over that day's lesson. I might say hello to someone, even Josiah, if he was having lunch there, but it was game time so I tried to stay focused on the task at hand. Then I would walk to the dime store and get myself a Diet Coke in a can—always in a can—to drink later during class and one mini Peppermint Pattie. I would eat the Peppermint Pattie on the walk to the drama building, which was directly across from the English department. I had an iPod that I filled up with various motivational rock songs and I'd listen to that on the walk across the quad. The last thing I would do until the students slumped into class at two was lie on the floor of my basement black-box theater teaching space and breathe. My goal was to let whatever was inside me rattle, hum, and bubble up to the surface. I had to apply to myself what I was about to teach about being open and available and ready to listen and respond. I had to be open to what the students would bring in and be flexible, so I could work with them. It's instinctual work, all about listening and responding. When they walked in I wanted to be alive, in a creative place and ready.

But before I started teaching I had to go through orientation as a new faculty member. Oberlin dedicates two full days to orientation right before the students arrive and it's required for all new faculty. This was really fun because Josiah was not new faculty anymore, so *he* had to stay home with the boys now, three years old and fifteen months old—a brutal age difference and time of life. Someone is always falling or hollering or needing to be changed. When you are taking care of small boys so close in age you are really in the trenches. But I got to put on the professor hat and bound out the door to get to a first meeting by 9 a.m.

Sometimes I rely excessively on being the funny, dumb blond actress, when I really am not. A first meeting at a new faculty orientation where I feel like an impostor anyway is a perfect place for me to get into the ditsy actress shtick, but it can work, so I did it. I made jokes about not having email until I was twenty-nine and fretted about what would happen if a student wanted to come over to the house. Would one make them dinner or not? It sort of broke the ice, and let the real professors ask the pressing, hard-core questions. At the end of the first meeting we all filed out the door to go to lunch in the environmental building, which was across the street from my new house. I was thinking of jetting home for a second to see how Josiah and the boys were faring when a lovely, slight, dark-haired woman came up to me.

"You must be Josiah Robinson's wife. I'm Sylvia."

8

Sylvia could have said she was Audrey Hepburn, because that is who she looked like and even sounded like, but Audrey Hepburn with an almost-French accent. That's a big compliment and if I knew then that she would in four months be living with my husband, I wouldn't have thought it, but I did think it at the time. I noticed her engagement ring right away because it had three good-sized diamonds on it. I had a big, yellow sapphire engagement ring that Josiah had given to me. It was huge, but Josiah said that was because it was "clown colored." It looked like a yellow Jolly Rancher set on its side. It was a marvelous ring, but Josiah really discouraged me from wearing it in academic settings. He didn't want people to think we had any money, which we really didn't, but if you did see my ring you might think otherwise.

Many generations ago my mother's side of the family was quite wealthy. A great-grandfather made lots of money as a banker, but during the next couple of generations nobody else struck gold. We have exhausted money. Meaning there isn't much left. Josiah's family also at one point had had a great deal of money but because of some bad luck also had seen a substantial financial downturn. So, the point is that both Josiah and I knew about nice things like travel, jewelry, good manners, and good upholstery. You could be fooled into thinking we were both loaded just by looking at the china that was in our sideboard or knowing the schools we had attended. But in truth, there wasn't tons of money around anymore. Everyone was fine, but no one was swimming in it.

But there was Sylvia wearing her substantial diamond ring. I liked that she was wearing it. I thought it was confident of her. She doesn't look like an academic. She wore all sorts of great designer clothes, which again I appreciated. In New York everybody looks great and is well dressed, but seeing someone in Ohio wearing Marc Jacobs is like spotting an owl in Central Park. Rare.

"I thought you were funny in there—everyone else is so serious," she said. Which of course I was flattered by, or relieved that I hadn't been seen as a fool, although in hindsight she might have thought I was a fool.

"Well, I am seriously wondering how I am going to pull off this teacher thing, but what the fuck, right? Here I am," I said. She laughed.

That's what is wild about this story. Sylvia seemed to really like me. She seemed to look up to me. (I was five years older than she, and about five inches taller.) She was a combination of needy and helpless and distant and self-contained. She was beguiling, I have to say, and she was funny, I might even give her hilarious at times. She said quite off-the-wall things, made good observations, and was very European. She smoked, but never smelled like it. Sylvia didn't call attention to herself and was quiet, but if you were paying attention you might hear her make a comment about the irony of being in Ohio, or the longevity of a turtle. Not snarky or mean, but smart and witty, and soft. I was thrilled to have a new would-be pal in town and welcomed the friendship right away.

"Hey—are you going to this lunch?" I asked.

"Yes," she said.

"Well, I live right down the street. Do you want to come over for a second? I want to check on the boys—and then you can see where we live. We just moved in."

"Oh, that would be great," she said enthusiastically.

I'm not kidding, it's like she was the freshman and I was the senior inviting her to come to my dorm room and try on clothes. I could feel my wing going up to take this sweet young thing under it and assure her everything would be all right in this weirdo, endearing town. I would make it all right for her. In a flash she became my new little project.

I thought our house was impressive and beautiful. It was done properly, from the high-gloss "celery" trim on the windows in the library to the Lulu DK striped fabric on the kitchen window seat. We wallpapered the back stairs and hallways—it looked like an orange grove. Leafy light and dark green branches with Ping-Pong ball–sized oranges nestled here and there. The floors and stairs were painted a cream color, but we left the original walnut banister untouched. I loved that hallway. I used to just go up there and sit in it and be proud of myself. Our kitchen was big and yellow. The painter—Billy—Josiah, and I created the yellow ourselves by dripping orange paint into a basic yellow for what seemed like an entire afternoon. It turned this heavenly deep, yolky Provençal yellow that we used upstairs in James's bedroom. It was such a great color we used it again downstairs in the living room and kitchen. We called it "James Yellow." The kitchen had an island in the middle with a downdraft stove and oven set in it. On the other side you could sit four people, the idea being that if friends came over we could all sit around and cook, eat, and drink together without someone being stuck alone in the kitchen. I also dreamed of the boys doing their homework there while I cooked supper. Everything was planned out for our big family life for the next twenty years. Anyone who walked in the doors could feel that. I'm sure Sylvia felt that.

"Oh, Isabel, this is beautiful. You must have worked so hard," she said as we walked up the stairs to the bedrooms. Josiah and the boys weren't home.

"Oh my God, we did. You should have seen Josiah—have you met him yet? Oh no, you met last spring, no? I'm sorry we missed him," I said.

"I did see him, just for a second at the department yesterday. Our offices are next door," she said.

"Oh, that's good. It's nice to be upstairs in that building." (Looking out for her at every turn . . .) "Anyway, he was so funny choosing the floors for the kitchen. I swear he becomes an expert at anything he takes on. He can tell the difference between an almond wood and a cherry from sixty yards away now. Such an academic, that one."

I could feel myself bragging about him. I often bragged about Josiah. It was easy to do—one, because I worshiped him and held him on a pedestal way above myself, and two, because he was naturally capable of doing small braggable things you could brag about. He could rewire lamps, which my mother *adored*. And he could needlepoint. He would needlepoint by the fire in reading glasses. He is big like a quarterback and square jawed, masculine, so it looked absurd to see him squint as he counted stitches. He would hum or mutter to himself in his baritone voice about lighter shades of teal as he finished a thread, like he was gay or a granny. It was amusing and sweet.

I took Sylvia all over the house discussing every fabric and door handle. I even changed in front of her in our bedroom. An awfully weird thing to do within forty-five minutes of meeting someone. I felt close to her right away. By the end of the visit I told her that she had, and must take me up on, a standing invitation to dinner every week. We picked Thursdays. I hated the thought of her in a lonely apartment while her brand-new husband was in New York. Josiah and I could offer her a practice home. One where there would be lots of food and children running underfoot. I wanted to share.

9

Josiah and I had become good friends with several couples our own age during the first year. One was Ward and Secca. Ward was Chinese and Secca was Japanese. Both of them taught in the English department. Both of them were twentieth-century people and knew a lot about modern culture. They taught courses like Los Angeles from Film to Poetry and Media in the Valley. Their house was filled with sleek gray furniture and kitschy West Coast lamps, and they had a cat with a Japanese name. Secca once told me a story about how her mother made her and her sister do a dance if they wanted juice. I thought it was the funniest image ever and have often since tried to get my boys to do a funny dance when they ask for juice. Ward and Josiah became close. They ran a poetry reading series together. And I always loved seeing Secca. She was such a lady. They were forever trying to find Asian ingredients to cook with. When they first came to Oberlin from California, they immediately went to Cleveland to find its version of Chinatown. They were disappointed when the

Cleveland Chinatown was really only a building. You would hear them planning a weekend trip to "China Building." It was funny. Then there was Rebecca and her husband, Sam. She taught nineteenth-century novels like *Emma* and *Pride and Prejudice* and looked like she had stepped out of that era. She was prudish and had bangs cut ever so slightly too short. She reminded me of Laura Ingalls Wilder. Apparently her mother had made all her clothes growing up and she didn't ever even kiss a boy until her senior year of high school. Her husband was a "floater." A floater is the name given to spouses who have followed their partners to a college where they have no job themselves. I was a floater until I landed my little course in the theater department. It's not an easy role. You have to come up with something to do, often in a remote location like Oberlin. Usually these people were doing "their own writing" or making pottery. You would find Sam endlessly gardening at their house while Rebecca worked herself to death trying to make tenure. They had no kids. Our three houses were two minutes away from one another.

There were other peripheral friends that we saw, but this was the core. And now Sylvia had joined our crew.

There were two women in Josiah's past who really gave me a pain in the neck. And since we fought about them a lot, I'm sure they gave Josiah a pain in the neck too. One was his first wife—whom I was just intimidated by. And the other was Edith, whom Josiah had had an affair with, putting the nail in the coffin of his first marriage. There is irony here because Josiah doesn't flirt or seem like a guy who would cheat at all. But at the end of the day, I guess he is the guy whose heart finds others while it is already committed. Still, I would bet that nine out of ten people would never guess he was that guy. I certainly didn't. I blamed the women. And I do get that it takes two to tango. That there is always a push and pull. I think it's shortsighted to think something is just one person's fault, that there is no cause and effect. But still I found it easier to blame the women.

Samantha, his first wife, had the reputation of being very smart but also a tad *difficile*. (My mother sometimes says certain words in French, like *difficile,* and now I guess I do too. There are just certain words that are more descriptive when said in French.) And she was defensive about everything. The lowdown on Samantha was that she caught Josiah in her web when he was a sophomore at Yale and she was a senior. She entangled him into a complicated relationship, and held him there until she got him to marry her when he was only twenty-four. That's how I heard it, anyway. I heard about fights lasting three weeks and how she would show up at Christmas in Atlanta where his father lived with his stepmother, Susan, and sulk. Susan said she was "no fun." And I loved that, because although I wasn't the brainiac Samantha was hailed to be, I was fun. But even though she was "no fun," Josiah's father and stepmother respected and liked her and always were in contact with her. That made me jealous. What plagued me was that I couldn't believe that one day Josiah wasn't going to wake up and realize that he had left a perfectly fine, wicked-smart woman who, if nothing else, lived with his son. The men in my family are from the don't-leave-the-mother-of-your-children school, so it made sense to me that one morning he would look at me and, no matter how much he loved me, would have to go and right what had been wronged. I got so sure of that sometimes that I would see an email that she had written him about travel times for their son and I'd pick a fight so that at the end of it I could confess that I was afraid he would leave me for her, and then he would convince me otherwise. Even when we had our own boys I was sort of paranoid that we would have to move to Texas. Now that I think about it, I was really inflexible about even the notion of moving to Texas, and it caused periodic tension. Samantha was short, slight, and had brown hair.

Then there was Edith. In my mind, Edith really was a freak show who had no sense of boundaries. My mother would call her a "shit stirrer." She and Josiah had managed, after the microblast that was his first divorce had calmed, to patch together a friendship. I don't know what the value of it was to either of them, and so it boiled down again and again to my belief that he should end their friendship since there was too much of a complicated past behind it. He refused. Edith would send him books and they would email about her ruinous relationships with men. She sent him huge letters. I mean physically large envelopes with drawings and doodles on them. I knew that trick because in high school that was my standby technique for charming a boy. Interesting doodles on the backs of envelopes. That she did it too drove me crazy. She even signed things "Love you." She did not even have the smarts to throw me a "Say hi to Isabel" bone. It infuriated me.

"My father and brother would *never* be such good friends with someone so spicy in their past! It's not fair! She is wildly flirting with you—and I just have to sit here and be cool with it because you are friends." I would put my hands up and do the quotation gesture when I said "friends." "Well, I'm not cool! Stop seeing her!" I would say in my most wifely, I've-had-it-up-to-here voice. One time in New York when I was six months pregnant with my first child, I was so mad about it I took my bare hands and squeezed a plateful of scrambled eggs and slow-baked tomatoes until I was sobbing on the floor with egg literally on my face. I found it humiliating that my husband would not give up a "friendship" with someone whom I saw as threatening, like a snake in our living room. I felt that he tortured me with her. But why would he do that? It was so ungentlemanly. I had given up endless friendships with men that I had been romantically involved with to make Josiah feel at ease (not that he ever asked me to or ever seemed all that threatened). And with none of them did I have an affair that ended a marriage. I didn't even tell him I went on two dates with Mick Jagger in L.A. because I didn't want to ruin the Rolling Stones for him. I thought it was what friends do for each other, and it hurt me so much that he wouldn't return the favor. Edith was small and had dark hair.

I wish I were the confident, cool person who can handle women from the past in an unruffled, grown-up, sophisticated way, but sadly I'm not. In my defense, though, I feel like, with the right woman, I could be. I have a made-up woman in my head whom I could handle. She would be tall and zaftig with long, red curly hair. She would have a big laugh and a habit of playing with your jewelry while you talked to her. Smart but not noticeably so. Just nice, maybe? But it's as if God is testing me with these complicated, dark-haired, petite chicks. I can't deal with them. I feel immediately dumb and as if I am going to trip over my own feet or spill my drink.

So here was another one on my doorstep, but this one was going to be my friend. There was simply no reason why I should be intimidated or wary of this woman even though she looked like Winona Ryder and her office was one wall away from my husband's. Now it seems pathetic, but I was so happy about the new friend thing that I initiated a ladies night for me, Sylvia, Rebecca, and Secca. It would take place on Tuesdays. We planned the first one for the second week of school, since we all needed a little time to get our classes going.

The orientation where I met Sylvia was midweek during the last week of August, and classes began the first week of September. The weekend in between was when Josiah covered the walls of our upstairs bathroom with the photographs. We were officially separated by the end of the term.

10

So the next month was the best month that I got in Ohio. We were not looking for a job or a house. I was not pregnant, and although it didn't amount to much, we had two salaries coming in. At night we would put our boys to sleep in their own, lovingly decorated rooms, cook dinner—which I swear to God we ate by candlelight in our new kitchen (very reminiscent of my parents, who to this day eat by candlelight every night). Or if we didn't do that we would go out with our gang of friends while an Oberlin student watched over the boys. By day we were teaching our classes or dealing with the daily life of the kids. We shopped at the farmers' market, bought doughnuts from the bakery in town, and went to concerts at the conservatory or antiwar sit-ins at the college (the Iraq war was in its third year). My life felt perfect.

There is a museum in Oberlin. It's small, but really good—just like everything there. Jim Dine (a painter I've always loved since I saw one of his *Robe* paintings in my best friend's parents' New York apartment) had a retrospective at this museum at the start of that second year. Dine is a monarch of modern art and because he paints lots of self-portraits and normal things like nails and bathrobes, I think he is easy to relate to. He and the curator filled up every inch of that museum with all the work of his life. The entire college turned out for the opening. In New York you probably would not bring the kids to an opening at a museum, but in Oberlin it would be strange if you didn't. We all put on our fancy duds and headed out to see the *Robes* and our friends.

It was mayhem. Dine's paintings literally went up the walls, stacked five high, so it didn't feel like a hushed museum usually does. Plus the place was jammed with everyone from the college. The boys ran around darting through people's legs. We would pick them up to see a portrait up close but then they would be gone again around some corner. Josiah and I easily fell into a tag-team setup where it's understood that one person will be a grown-up while the other chases kids, and then after a reasonable amount of time you switch. There were people there that we had not seen all summer, so there was a lot of hugging and what my mother would call "patati-patata," nonimportant chat.

"Hello, Isabel! Are you back? Are you moved in? How was Maine? Look at your boys! So sweet! I hear you are teaching! Well done! I see Josiah is doing a reading next week—must go to that."

Lots and lots of that. All very lovely and normal. I would then answer, and ask the usual follow-up questions.

"Oh, it was lovely, thank you. I'm so excited to be

teaching. Who knew it was so hard to write a syllabus? . . . And you? How was Ireland? You teach there in the summer, yes? Heaven . . . Did you get to travel much? Are you on sabbatical this semester? What will you be working on . . . ?" Et cetera . . .

But I could notice that James was missing in the sea of people or I would see Wallace pulling on a canvas and then I would be able to excuse myself quickly and move on.

During a minisearch for James (he never really got that far away) I turned a corner into a smaller gallery and there was Josiah talking to Sylvia. It struck me right away that they were standing one inch too close to each other. It was nothing more than a quick feeling that registered fleetingly somewhere in my gut. I'm not even sure if the feeling had time to make its way up to my brain, but if it did, I instantly ignored it.

"Oh, Bully, there you are! I think our children are going to destroy all of Jim Dine's life's work if we don't head out of here soon," I said.

And then I am pretty sure I linked arms with Sylvia and complimented her on her dress that had embroidered birds and flowers on it.

"God, is that pretty! Where does one find something like that? Don't you love that, Josiah?" I swear, I teed her up constantly to him. I really did think she was funny, but I always pointed out her sense of humor to Josiah.

"Oh, that is funny, Sylvia. Didn't you think that was funny, Josiah? Lumpish? What a word, and it's exactly what he is like!"

I felt sorry for her because her husband was in New York and she didn't have children, a fabulous house, and a marvelous man, like I had. I wanted to make her feel good about herself.

"Hey, girls night is Tuesday, but do you want to go running with me tomorrow around Tappan Square? We can just do it twice and then I'll show you the only place to get a pedicure in town," I said.

"Oh, that would be great. I haven't done my toes since last May," she said in her diluted French accent.

"Wait—didn't you get married in July?" I said.

And then she put her head down and said, "I am ashamed to say I had terrible feet when I got married."

Well, I did think that was bizarre. Didn't all people who wore Prada (of course that is what the embroidered bird dress was) have the good sense to get their toes done before they got married? Isn't that part of the fun of getting married, to get your toes done with your pals? What if she didn't have any pals to do her toes with? But didn't she say she had sisters? Then I really started to feel sorry for her. It's not like she said, "Oh, I don't give a shit about pedicures, so I didn't get my toes done before my wedding." She said, "I am *ashamed* to say I didn't get my toes done before I got married." I thought it was an extraordinary statement.

"Well, don't get too excited, it's not Estée Lauder, but they do a nice job and it will be some good girl-time for us. You'll watch the boys, right, Josiah? Don't tell me you have to go to the library on a Sunday," I said.

"Sure," he said. "Maybe the boys and I will go hunting or watch football." Josiah had no interest in sports at all. We all laughed, but I couldn't help feeling like he felt left out.

Sylvia and I did go running and get our toes done the

next day. She told me about her family. She is half French and half American. She grew up in Vermont with her mother and two sisters. She said her father and mother were still married, but when they were growing up he lived in a different town because he was working somewhere else. I asked her if that had been hard and she calmly replied no, that it was fine, that somehow it had worked for them. I thought it was odd that she had so little feeling about her father, who lived apart from her for times while she grew up; I am so invested in "the family." I had had dinner almost every night with my parents and brother around the dining room table. I had memories of touch football games in the country and driving in the car listening to the Doobie Brothers, all together. Is it really a family if you don't spend lots and lots of time together and if you don't live together? But she didn't seem bothered by it and I didn't push it. Again, when I look back on it, I had very specific ideas about what marriage and family were. When people do it differently, even though intellectually I understand that there are many ways to slice an onion, inside I just think that the way my family did it is the nice way to do it. My parents adore each other. My mother once said they are the happiest if they can spend the entire day together. They seemed connected, we all felt connected. When one member of our family leaves, someone yells, "Constant contact!" The feeling is, it's nicer to be together. So that's how I think a family should be. That's how we did it. I am aware that I, like my mother, tend to think there is only one way to do things. The fact is, it's rare that a person is just flat-out wrong about something. At the time I second-guessed Sylvia's ease with her seemingly disjointed family.

I couldn't believe anyone would be so cool about their parents living apart.

On the way home, after our run, I was telling Sylvia about each little store on one of the two streets that had stores, and what you could find in there.

"That place looks like a terrible knickknack store with bad-smelling potpourri and dried flowers and it is, *except* that they have these great wineglasses. The whole store is a disaster area and then they have these beautiful thin glasses." She nodded.

"Have you been to Agave? It's Dan's, who owns Black River, second place. The best burrito I have ever had. You can get everything in them and they have this chipotle sauce that is divine. A must. We eat there three times a week." She nodded. (It turned out that I ended up eating many meals with Sylvia and she is no salad eater—she can pack it in. Another thing that impressed me about her.)

"That bead store actually has some cool earrings but the clothes are horrid and all look like they are for larger women. I think you can take jewelry making, though—maybe we should do that one day?" She nodded.

"The health food store has good bread and lots of organic graham crackers and things. It's wildly expensive, but I shop there to support the place." She nodded.

"Isabel." We were stopped in front of the conservatory where a ten-year-old faculty kid with shoulder-length hair was playing the fiddle. "I think you are amazing."

"Wow—thanks." I loved how she gave me these huge compliments. But now that I look back, perhaps she just felt sorry for this woman who was showing off and seemed to need huge compliments.

"You got pulled out of New York and into this tiny town, which, no matter how much you do love it and say it has everything, is really a tiny town in the middle of nowhere . . . to follow your husband, and you have such a positive attitude about it. You have some great karma coming your way."

"Wow—well, yeah. But I gotta say, I feel like I already have the good karma because I have such a nice life. Who wouldn't want to follow Josiah to a great town to raise kids and live in my house? I feel really lucky." I meant it.

What I was doing was trying to lead by example. I wanted her to stay in the town with me and get her husband to come and live there. He was an actor in New York whom I had never heard of. I couldn't imagine that he would be leaving some big career. I wanted to show her that you could make a life—a good life—in the wilds of Ohio. We could make our own cool city, where we could teach what we wanted, be progressive politically, eat organically from our friend's restaurants, live in cheap, beautiful houses and have many dinner parties in them, raise our babies together, all of whom would learn violin by the age of six with the Suzuki method that was taught at the conservatory. As a group, the faculty children I met in Oberlin were some of the most well-behaved, charming, and sweet children I have ever come across. No spoiled brats in that neck of the woods.

I thought if she admired me so much, maybe Sylvia would try and copy me into motherhood and domesticity and then I would have a good friend my own age built into the little paradise I was creating for us. That was my plan.

11

I can't remember fighting with Josiah that month of September. I remember other fights from years past, mostly about Edith and drinking and sometimes money. Josiah has a hard time with drinking. I can't say he is worse off than many other people I know, but in my mind, he is one of those people who really shouldn't drink. Periodically he goes for years and years without drinking at all. He quit drinking during his first year at Yale so he could work harder and didn't drink again for seven years. When he would start again he would be all right for a while but then it would get to be too much and it could be very dark. We fought about that a lot, but not at this time in our lives. He had not had a drink since James was six weeks old.

James was born in Cambridge. He was born in May and although I don't like Cambridge for the most part, May really is lovely there. I had James naturally, no drugs. That might have been because I had been brainwashed by all the worthy women in that town who don't use drugs and have doulas deliver their babies in their backyards, or because the nurse in the prelabor room looked me in the eye and challenged me to do it, or because I wanted to show off. Whatever reason I had, Josiah and my doctor were not in favor of the idea. Too much pain and why? But I thought I wanted to and no man in Cambridge would dare tell a woman in labor what to do with her body, so I won. Sort of. It was insanely painful, but more than that it was so ugly and loud. At one point I was on my knees facing backward, holding on to the top of the bed with my ass waving around in the air, and hollering. I just think it was too much. James got sort of stuck with his umbilical cord over his shoulder so it took longer than the tough-as-nails nurse in the waiting room estimated. It was just a lot of me gone wild. I always thought Josiah should have been a medical doctor because he is so smart and good at bodily functions and blood. He knows what he is looking at when he sees the sonograms. He shocks the technicians by pointing out the fetus's liver or pancreas. So I thought he of all people would be able to handle me in natural childbirth. But the reality of it is that I think I grossed him out. I hate to say that, and it's only a theory, but I think it's true. I have a friend who thinks we should go back to the fifties, when the men had to stay in the waiting room instead of getting a front-row seat, and I can see her point. In the waiting room they are worried and thinking about you. They can picture you as their heroine, valiantly escorting their precious baby into the world. In their imagination, your mouth might be firmly closed, you might have a determined look in your eyes. You are not a cross-eyed, screaming wildebeest. Not only will you look better in their imagination but this will be the image they hold on to for all eternity. When they are in there with you, suddenly it turns into how they feel, their experience, the fact that they are hungry or uncomfortable in the chair. And they get grossed out by the fact that you just took a dump where their kid is about to come out.

In any case, not that he ever said anything to me about it, I always have felt that Josiah got turned off by James's birth. Not by James, he adores James, but by me.

James came out eventually and was funny, moony, and wonderful from the very first hours. He was born, weighing in at exactly eight pounds, on Cinco de Mayo. A day when it seems the entire world has fun.

As soon as James was six weeks old and I wasn't bleeding anymore, we left Cambridge to spend the summer in Maine and eventually head out to Oberlin for the first time. My father came down to drive Wallace, James, Plover (the dog, a sweet Norfolk terrier who looks like an alive teddy bear), and me up to Maine. Josiah was going to stay in Cambridge, send off the movers to Ohio, and drive up there in my father's car the following day. We swapped Dad's jeep for our family minivan, as the minivan had the car seats.

Somehow in between the moment when he closed the door of our crappy little brown house and when he headed up the Mass Turnpike the next morning, Josiah got very drunk in a bar next to MIT called the Miracle of Science. It was a bar he used to frequent in grad school. I called him from Maine before I went to bed with our two tiny children, and he was just smashed, still at the bar and crying about leaving Cambridge. I had thought he was going to eat Indian food and go to my brother's house around six that evening. So there was lying involved and driving my father's car and it was just bad. I made him leave the bar, with me on the cell phone, and drive to David's house. I was undone. There I was in my parents' house in Maine, nursing and up all night with a six-week-old baby and dealing with his jealous, pissed-off two-year-old brother, and Josiah was blotto driving across the Mass. Ave. bridge to pass out in my older brother's house.

It seems so clear to me now that although Josiah loved us and wanted dearly to have a nice family, there was something in him that just did not want to let him do it. Like Dr. Jekyll and Mr. Hyde. That's why it was so hard to figure out. When he wanted it, he was on board 100 percent; it was so pure and sweet. When he didn't, it was dark and destructive. It was hard to tell that he was the same person. And it was hard to tell when he was going to be himself and when that dark guy would take over. By this point in our marriage I was beginning to understand that he was complex, maybe too complex for the amount we had taken on, but it was hard to accept. However, I really believed he loved me and the boys and wanted more than anything to stay together as a family. I told him on the phone never to drink again, to choose our family, which had just gotten bigger. Then I waited through the night.

The next day when he got out of the car in our driveway in Maine and swore on our sons that he would never drink another sip of alcohol again, for us, I believed him and loved him even more for choosing that path. I couldn't bear to think about what life would be if he didn't choose us.

12

Back to Oberlin.

It's important to understand how much we all saw one another. It's the great part about a small academic town and could be seen as the worst possible part. I love to be close to everything. The fact that I could yell out my bedroom window and Josiah could hear me in his office was worth the price of admission. I loved the fact that I would see Sylvia in the bookstore and then twenty minutes later in the café and then two hours later walking home, when we would make plans to see each other again either later on in the evening or the next day. If I wasn't teaching I was with the boys. They too were in constant contact with Josiah and with our friends. Everyone knows your kids in Oberlin. The students know them, the faculty knows them, and all the shopkeepers know them. It all feels very safe. Very cozy. Of course this means that everyone knows almost everything about you. Not only are you interacting with the same twenty people day in and day out, but you live next door to them. You can see one another through the windows. In our new house, we lived next door to two dance professors. I could see at night how long it took them to drink a bottle of wine at dinner. I didn't mean to notice but my window in the kitchen looked into their kitchen/dining room. So as I got supper ready I could see them opening the bottle of wine and as I washed the dishes I could see how far down the wine had gone in the bottle where it sat on the table. You don't want to be nosey, but you can't help it. No one can help it. If your mother is in town for the weekend, people know. If you hang a new swing in your backyard, people know. If you forget to put out your recycling one week, people know. There is nowhere to hide. But hiding is the last thing I do. I have no secrets. I have lain in bed at night searching my soul for one little secret that I have about myself and I can't find it. I'd tell the bus driver I had hemorrhoids if he ever asked. It's just how I have always been. I'm not sure that a secret is even safe with me.

Secrets were the very subject of conversation at girls night the second time we gathered. On this particular week, Secca, Rebecca, Sylvia, and I had chosen to have our dinner at Too Chinoise, the only Chinese restaurant in town. I am not lying when I say that I have never had such good Chinese food in New York as there is at this joint in Oberlin. Like the other two good restaurants in town, it was started by a former Oberlin student. They had delicious orange chicken, and all the shrimp dishes were outstanding. The place was really good.

It was a balanced and interesting girls night group. On one hand, none of us had any real choice about who was there. It's like that expression "You can pick your friends but you can't pick your family." But in Oberlin you can't really pick your friends, you just get who you get. On the other hand, we felt like we had lucked out. It was amazing that we all spanned the same decade in age. I was the only one at the table with kids, which made me feel better about the fact that I was the only one at the table without a Ph.D.

The group was out of central casting. Secca had those old-fashioned Japanese looks, but she wore very current, mod clothes. Very black hair, lovely almond eyes, and she often wore red matte lipstick. She looked like the best representation of a certain kind of Japanese stereotype. Rebecca was fresh faced and Midwestern looking. Imagine an academic milkmaid. Sylvia, as I have mentioned, was just shy of the movie-star version of a French dark-haired actress—Irene Jacob meets Natalie Portman. She was always dressed beautifully. Because I was on the cover of *Seventeen* magazine when I was fourteen and I am an actress, I depend on the fact that, objectively, I am good-looking. Tall, blond hair, odd looks but undeniably attractive. But I can tend to depend too much on the idea that I am pretty and sometimes, I don't try very hard. If I put the effort into the mascara and clothes it can be good, but if I don't, especially as I age, I can look homely. I also thought that because I was married and had had my babies, I didn't have to try as hard in the looks department . . . stupid.

I was the one who brought up secrets. I happen to think there are two kinds of people in the world: people who have secrets and people who don't. I asked the group if they had any.

I figured my pals were women, and smart women at

that, and I could really cook up a good conversation if I pushed a little. It was a girls night after all. I like organized dinner conversation that feels almost like a parlor game. Going around the table answering questions like, "Where would you live if you didn't live where you live now?" Or, "If you could change one thing about yourself what would it be?" Some people deplore being put on the spot, or just think whoever is in charge is controlling. My family is of the go-around-the-table camp. When I was growing up, we had something we played at dinner every night called show and tell. Everyone in the family and any guests would have to tell what they did all day. Whoever was home first starts and recalls the day, highlighting transportation, interesting phone calls, and meals. I can hear my mother now:

"Well, I had wonderful transportation because the B train came right away and I got a seat and then at Seventh Avenue, I hopped over to the E that was waiting and it zipped me right over to Fiftieth and Lexington. Marvelous."

As we were growing up, the ritual served two important purposes: our parents got to hear what we had done during the day and we got to hear what they did.

But it wasn't just show and tell, we also went around the table and answered questions like, "Who would you vote for if the election was today?" Or, "What was the best and worst of the summer?" A dinner without a little planned-out conversation ahead of time makes me feel very disorganized.

It's hard to write in retrospect because I can't remember if I thought then what I think now. I wonder, did

Sylvia inspire me to ask questions like, "Do you have any secrets?" I knew very well that she was the kind of person who did—but I wanted to probe. Why? Did I have some premonition that she would eventually hold one of the biggest secrets one can have, that she was in love with my husband? My grandmother was said to be psychic. Am I? I believe that women know lots of information about other women, especially about a woman who is involved with their man in some way. Sixth sense? Instincts? During this time I had the instincts of an animal. A dog or something, like I was being driven by gut and nature alone.

When I asked the women's group at dinner about secrets, Rebecca blushed. I think she thought I was going to follow up by asking something about vibrators or porn. Secca said she was a good secret keeper and that she had a million secrets. No surprise there. Sylvia gave me a look out of the corner of her eye and avoided the subject by listening intently to everyone else's answers, taking her time to ask more soft-spoken questions about what anyone else had said.

I then blurted out, "I have no secrets, but sometimes I think I could be nicer to Josiah. Sometimes I think I am a bitch to him, and I wish I wasn't. It's the kids and I'm exhausted and cooking and cleaning all the time, but still he doesn't deserve what a cow I am to him sometimes." Again, I let go of a secret before I even recognized that it was a secret. I wanted to open up and confess that my marriage wasn't always as perfect as it looked. Test the waters to see if these were real friends you could trust with marital warts. See if this was going to be a real women's group where we would air our feelings and bond over the common struggles and joys of marriage. Josiah made me feel badly about our fights. And I did feel badly that we fought, but I also thought it was explainable. Who didn't fight if they had two small kids, not a lot of money, two jobs, car seats, and not much opportunity for sex or trips or alone time? Didn't all parents in their thirties fight? It certainly looked like all the couples in the supermarkets and zoos were tired and fighting. I thought we were normal, but Josiah made me feel that if I got furious at him for not remembering to pay the credit card bill I was out of control and had anger issues. But doesn't everyone get angry if there are creditors on your ass? I opened the discussion to the girls, thinking I was safe. Thinking we were all on the same side. Thinking that I might get some helpful advice. And just at the key moment when they could have looked at me like I was nuts and a bad wife, Sylvia said, "Sometimes I don't think I'm so nice to Jeff either."

Ahhh, I thought, solidarity.

13

Jeff. Jeff was Sylvia's new husband who lived in New York. Sylvia rarely spoke about Jeff. She referred to him so rarely I sometimes forgot she was married. I am someone who every four seconds drops the sentence "My husband is waiting in the car" or "I'll have to talk to Josiah, my *husband,* about that." I love saying the word *husband.* But not Sylvia.

I used to talk to Josiah about it. "Hey, do you think it's weird that Sylvia never talks about Jeff?"

"She does."

"Really? Even when I specifically ask her about him at girls night, I can't get a straight answer."

"It's probably complicated. They just got married, she came out here . . . who knows what goes on between two people."

"Yeah, but isn't it weird that he hasn't come out here yet? I would be going crazy if I had to be separated from you so soon after we got married."

Now at this point in the story, when I picture this kind

of conversation, I imagine that I was snuggled up to Josiah on the sofa with no reading material, but he was probably sitting straight up reading something. Josiah was always reading something. That was true from the moment I met him—I think I even remember him as a boy reading on the dock. But by this time in our marriage the reading had gotten out of control. He would read something on his way to reading something else. Two years before this he might not have been reading, and the conversation on the sofa might have gone like this:

"Bully," I would say.

"Yes, Bully," he would say, looking in my eyes.

"Do you notice that Sylvia never talks about Jeff?"

"She does, I think." He might kiss me there.

"She doesn't. And I think it's strange because they just got married." I would definitely have kissed him there.

"Maybe she's made him up, the freaky, mysterious little eighteenth centurist!" he would say.

I would laugh there.

"But, Bully, if I was separated from you so soon after we got married, I would be miserable and never stop talking about you."

"But, my Bully, we would never be separated because we are the Bullys."

"I know. I hate being separated."

"No separations," he would say.

"No." And then we would kiss a lot more. We often told each other that we would never be parted and would always be together. But that fall, things got ever so slightly cooler. Almost undetectable at first.

Jeff did end up coming to Oberlin in mid-September

and Josiah and I had a dinner party for him and Sylvia. Jeff was slight and fair. It turned out that he was actually Sylvia's second cousin, and like Josiah and me, they had known each other as children. Their families were close. At the dinner party it was very noticeable that he was besotted with her and that she was mezzo mezzo about him. They were odd bedfellows. She was dressed up as if she were going to Anna Wintour's for dinner and he looked more like the waiter coming to work at the party before he changed into his uniform. I was wearing all black, and a large gold bracelet my mother-in-law had given me. It had been hers and you could tell she bought it in the eighties. It was a wide cuff and had a lightning bolt cut out of the center of it. If I had had two I would have looked like Wonder Woman.

When they arrived Sylvia introduced me to Jeff, whom I made a big deal about.

"Isabel, I love your bracelet. You really know how to wear a bracelet," she said.

That made me feel so cool! She had identified me as the kind of woman who knew how to wear a bracelet. Was it true? Who knows, I had just slapped the thing on so I wasn't wearing just black, but she made me feel like I had a knack, or just loads of taste. She also said it like she had no fucking idea how to wear a bracelet, which, given what she was wearing and how carefully she always accessorized, she clearly did. But that was her deal, compliment me and appear to undermine herself at the same time. Build me up.

I can't even remember what Jeff looked like because he was so unassuming. I sat next to him and tried to make him feel better about his acting career that was going nowhere and about how happy I was that Sylvia had come to town. Josiah and Sylvia were at the other end of the table chatting away, almost touching heads. Ward and Secca and Rebecca and Sam were in the middle. I had made vinegar chicken with chard. Sounds awful, but it's wonderfully perfect for an early chilly autumn night. I served it on our prettiest plates, which we had gotten for our wedding from Josiah's mother, possibly my most beloved material possession. They were purple and green ironstone dishes from James II and we had eight.

After dinner when Josiah and I were cleaning up we discussed at length what a mismatch Sylvia and Jeff were.

"It's just bizarre!" I said. Having had four glasses of wine, I probably was being overly dramatic and hyperbolic. "Is he even smart? She's so smart and pretty. What is she doing with *him*? They don't even seem like they are from the same world! And they are *cousins*?" I slurred.

"Second cousins and they didn't know each other that well as children," he said soberly, because he was sober.

"I know, but come on! There are so many people to marry besides your cousin."

"I guess there was pressure from their families."

"What? Like an arranged marriage? She's from Vermont."

"No, I think she just felt like she had to marry him because they had been together for some time," he said defensively.

"How do you know that? Is that what you two were talking about at dinner?" I said, really trying not to sound jealous because I wasn't.

"No, no, we just talk about it sometimes. She's my friend."

"She's my friend."

"I think their marriage is complicated."

"Well, that sucks, because they just got married."

"Yeah."

14

I was not the obvious candidate to be a teacher. As a girl, I had terrible dyslexia. I tried awfully hard and loved school, but I got bad grades. Really bad grades. I recall on a math test that I actually got a 14. My math teacher, Mr. Olvidas, who was wildly attractive and I think had a little inappropriate crush on me, looked at me as he handed back the exam with a big 14 circled in red like it hurt his feelings to have to give it to me.

Anyway, it surprised me to find out that I loved teaching. Luckily I was not teaching math but acting. The best part about acting is the imagination part. In your imagination you can do anything, feel anything, live through anything. Imagination is the key, in many people's opinion, to being a good actor. So that semester, essentially, I was teaching ten seniors in the theater department how to imagine. The imagination is like a muscle. Once you start using it, it gets stronger and more flexible—it becomes readily available. The other thing I was teaching was instinct. How to act on your instincts.

"React! React! React!" I would chant in class.

"Take in what the other person is doing and react. Don't think. Listen and respond!" It's Sanford Meisner technique and it's quite effective for people who are open and available to it. The Meisner technique derives from the teachings of Stanislavski, the Russian actor and theater director, who was the granddaddy of most European and American naturalistic acting. Meisner was his student and eventually he developed his own technique, which encourages the actor to work moment to moment, developing an ability to improvise within the scene using personal responses instead of relying on what is scripted. I was trying to squeeze everything I'd learned in an almost three-year study at the William Esper Studio into a twelve-week class, but the principles are still the same. When you are in the two-year training everyone tells you not to have a relationship or take an acting job because the work is too raw, and when you start to play with your imagination everything gets unearthed and mixed up and you become very emotional and slightly unhinged. That's the advice for the student. If you're the teacher you should have your shit together enough to realize your imagination is just a tool and so is using your instinct to create a certain behavior. Yes, you may be able to imagine something as horrifying as your child being hurt in an ungodly accident, but you have the skill and wherewithal to get yourself out of that fantasy just as quickly. I felt confident that I was able to teach this material without getting overly emotional or unhinged. But I was talking three times a week for two hours, about daydreaming, imagining the worst possible scenario or the best possible scenario, and using instincts.

Maybe as a result my instincts were sharpening. I think I was hyper in tune with the human condition. This is what I sounded like in class:

"If you need to produce behavior onstage or in a movie it must be real. It must come from someplace truthful in you. Specific and truthful. I don't care where you get the emotion. If you need to be in life-ending, sobbing tears at the close of the play you must get there by producing real behavior. How do you get that behavior? By imagining. Imagine your dog gets hit by a car and dies in your arms on the side of the road. Imagine you are speaking at your mother's funeral. Imagine your husband is in love with your sister. How would it make you feel?"

Three times a week I would rant at these kids. The kids who started off full of themselves and closed up started to come alive. They were resistant at first but when they started to let the work play on them they got so excited and proud of themselves. Watching people live through a human emotion that they conjured themselves is breathtaking. They can't believe that they have done it. They are scared at first but they soon start to crave the rush of scaring themselves or making themselves cry tears of joy. It's a privilege to get to see it and an honor to get to teach it.

Between the teaching, my family, my house, my new friends, and our new town, I felt like life was finally going my way. I vividly remember one walk I had on the way home from class. There were real streets and sidewalks in Oberlin, but there were also lots of littler winding paths that took you from one building or dorm to another. I could get all the way home on those paths without taking a proper sidewalk. On that day, I remember thinking that my life was perfect. It felt so perfect that I thought something was bound to go wrong. Life doesn't stay this good. I thought that Josiah's father would probably have a heart attack. Or maybe my parents would get in a car crash. My worries were all about the generation above us. I just thought that the other shoe would drop. I remember exactly where I was on the path. I was passing the environmental center. I remember because there's a pond next to it where my boys looked for frogs. I thought that the pond would soon freeze and I worried about what would happen to the frogs. I seemed to remember that maybe they froze too in some sort of hibernation. Was that right? Would the boys ask me? Could we make a project out of it and ask the professors in the environmental center? It was a wonderful place to have a family and raise children, I thought as I walked by. But then I suddenly knew something was about to go wrong. And it did.

15

Josiah and I had season tickets to the opera. When you teach at the college you get major discounts at the conservatory for the season's productions. Professors may get paid well under a hundred grand a year, but if you take advantage of the little perks here and there you start not to feel so bad about that number. You get to go to art openings and have the entire summer off. The opera on Sunday was *La Bohème* but I just didn't feel like going.

"Do you think we can get Grace to come and babysit for the opera on Sunday?" Josiah said.

"Ohhhhhhh, the opera," I said. One of my New Year's resolutions, other than accepting water anytime someone offered it to me, was to take advantage of living on a college campus. And going to the opera would certainly fall into that category.

"We don't have to go," he said.

"No, no, we do. We should," I said.

And then I said something that I would spend the rest of my life questioning why I did.

"Why don't you take Sylvia? Sundays are so lonely. Take Sylvia."

"Are you sure?"

"Yes. I want to spend some time with the boys before this big week of teaching—take Sylvia."

"All right, I'll ask if she can go," he said.

This conversation took place on Friday afternoon. On Saturday night Sylvia, Josiah, and I drove to Cleveland together and saw a play that George from the theater department was in. It was a regional production of *Urine-town*. I couldn't stand the play, it didn't matter that the production was better than fine. In my opinion nothing puts people in a worse mood than bad theater. Everyone feels resentful of the wasted time and then guilty because clearly people have put a big effort into it.

Sylvia came over to our house because we were going to drive together. We had to move the children's car seats from the minivan so that Sylvia could sit in the second row and not the third. When you remove a car seat that belongs to a three-year-old, what you find under it is revolting. Thousands of old dried Cheerios, probably some caked-on spilled milk, four pieces of Lego, a map. I would love to meet the family who somehow can keep that underworld clean, but I'm sure it doesn't exist.

"Oh, what the fuck, Isabel, this is disgusting," Josiah said as he lifted the car seat onto the driveway.

"Sorry," I said. It hurt my feelings that he was blaming me, but at the same time I pathetically felt guilty for not being the Supermom that keeps that world of grossness under control.

"It's just . . . look at all this shit." He was really upset and started madly cleaning the seat.

"Relax, it's not that bad," I said defensively.

"It's just slovenly," he said.

Slovenly. Tears shot to my eyes. Slovenly was a low blow coming from Josiah, who was much neater than I was. He could have said messy, or even piggish, but slovenly felt mean to me. I turned around and left Josiah in the fading light in the driveway wiping the seat clean with paper towels for Sylvia. I crossed the back lawn heading to the kitchen door, where Sylvia was sitting with the boys and the sitter while they ate their supper. The door was open and I could see my blond little guys dutifully spooning chicken soup into themselves. I wasn't slovenly. Life with children is messy. Josiah had hurt my feelings.

We ended up being late to the play. And I guess in the first scene George had a big number. But I didn't know that because we were late. So afterward when we were gushing untruthfully about how much we loved the play, he asked what we thought of the first "number." He was a real musical theater nut and used words like *number* all the time. I said without thinking about it that we had missed it because we were late. Well, our friend took big offense to that and proceeded to go off the rails with hurt feelings, saying that if I really cared about him as a friend or, for that matter, for theater as an art form, I would never be so rude as to be late.

Rude? So now I am rude and slovenly. It was all I could do not to burst into tears then, and I actually did in the car on the drive home. The three of us talked about how bad the play was the entire hour-long ride home.

We dropped Sylvia off at her apartment. It was the first time I saw where she lived. I was so exhausted and daunted by how late it was, all I wanted was for Sylvia to get out so I could go home with my husband, but before she did she and Josiah had a little conversation about the next day.

"So should we meet there?" she said, leaning forward into the front seat like a kid.

Josiah got overly polite at this point.

"Oh, well, or I could pick you up? I have the tickets," he said.

Pick her up? That was weird.

"Oh, no," she said, getting the weirdness of his offer.

"We'll meet there," he said. This conversation was starting to annoy me.

"Okay—well, now that that is figured out, thanks for coming to that fucking terrible show, Sylvia," I said. "Sorry I cried."

"Oh, don't worry," she said, trying to figure out the childproof sliding door. I think she felt badly for me that I was having a hard time.

"Good night," we all said at the same time, and she ran up the stairs into her building.

Josiah and I didn't talk about anything in particular after that. We got home to our pretty brick house, paid the sitter, and went to bed.

16

I hate Sundays. I get the Sunday blues just like my mother. She always warned me that if I ever felt bad about something on a Sunday or something bad happened on a Sunday, wait until Monday to deal with it because more than likely the majority of the shittiness was just because it was Sunday. Her antidote to Sunday blues, and anything else for that matter, is to take a bath.

I knew that this particular Sunday was going to be extra long because Josiah would be at a three-hour opera in the afternoon and I would have the task of entertaining the children solo in a town that felt particularly empty on Sunday because everything was closed and the students were all asleep. I decided to take the boys to the Carlyle Nature Conservancy just outside of town. There is a sugar bush there where in the spring you can watch maple syrup being made by people in Colonial dress (who get a little carried away as those reenactment actors tend to get). You can also hold a snake and feed an owl. It has a small aviary with all the birds that are native to Ohio.

They take wounded birds and house them. They have Ohio turtles and groundhogs. It's all about nature in Ohio. There are trails through the woods and a tree house to climb in. The little ones love it. It's a soothing and beautiful place. During the day, I must have been distracted by the children because I didn't think about Josiah and Sylvia at the opera. I was timing my return to be slightly after when I thought the opera would be out, so when I came home Josiah would be there to help me unload the boys from the car. He might have even started their supper. I was picturing him taking the baton and me sinking into a hot bath with the Sunday paper. But when we pulled into the driveway the house was dark.

I unloaded the boys one at a time. James by this point could walk but in the dark it was just easier to carry him into the house. Then I got Wallace out, watched him run in, narrowly avoiding tripping on the flagstones that we still needed to put into the earth. Then I got the diaper bag and pulled two milky sippy cups out from under the passenger seat. Once in the house, I put a video on for the boys and sat in the kitchen thinking that at any second Josiah would walk in the door. When he didn't I couldn't believe it, and I started getting the Annie's mac and cheese out of the cupboard to make the kids' supper. And as the water was starting to boil, I heard the front door open.

"Sorry, sorry, sorry!" he said, rushing into the kitchen with his hands up.

"Mea culpa! My God that was a time disaster! Bully, I'm sorry. The opera was an hour longer than I thought and it was swarming with students that accosted me about their papers. I'm truly sorry," he said. It was such a big apology and he looked so sweet and earnest, all my madness went away.

"Bully—you were there for one hundred years," I said, falling into his arms.

"I know. Awful. Go take a bath. I've got the boys," he said.

Relieved that he was home and touched that he knew I would want a bath, I went upstairs. We put the boys to bed, ate Chinese food in front of the TV, and went to bed. We never even talked about Sylvia. What we did talk about was our friend Scott.

Scott had been teaching at Oberlin on a "one year" the year before. He was slightly younger than us and married to a woman I never met because she was finishing her Ph.D. at U of Pitt the entire year he was in Oberlin. He would drive there every weekend to be with her and their huge Burmese mountain dog named Troy. He had since gotten a teaching position at Pittsburgh and so they were finally together.

"Bully, you are never going to believe this awful story," Josiah said.

"What?" I said, riveted. Josiah rarely had big gossipy stories to tell me. He wasn't that way.

"Scott and Marni are separated," he said.

"What!" I said.

"Scott was feeling weird about Marni, so he Googled the word *love* on her computer, and tons of love emails came up between Marni and their best friend out there, Trent," he said.

"Oh my God—you can Google someone's email?"

"Yeah, somehow you can."

"That is incredibly horrible. Poor Scott . . ."

"I know—brutal."

"That is so fucked up—he just got there. Were they seeing each other last year?"

"I don't know. We barely got a chance to speak. He is in a really dark place and really upset."

"I'll bet. Maybe he should come stay with us. Is he teaching?"

"I offered, but he is teaching and then there is Troy—that dog is so big."

"Jesus," I said, and then I thought for a second.

"Bully. This is going to sound terrible, but don't you think Sylvia and Scott would be a good couple?"

"What? No—Sylvia is married."

"Oh, I know, but she never talks about her husband—I don't think she is very happy with her marriage."

"Well, it's complicated, and I don't think we should get into it," he said. His tone changed.

"No, you are right. I just got carried away. Wow—poor Scott, he worshiped that Marni."

17

At that point in the semester I was teaching *The Spoon River Anthology.* It's a book of poems, really, but it's used in the Meisner technique for character work. The poems are used as monologues, but they are not your average-bear monologues, because they are poems. I don't think there is anything more fun than talking shop with your husband. If I got stuck, I would ask Josiah's advice on the meaning of the poems, and we would talk about how it fit into my teaching. It was a blast. I was for once in his arena and could hold my own. It was a chance for him to see me strut my stuff. It felt like somebody else's world but it was ours. I loved it.

That week I was introducing the *Spoon River* monologues. It was hard material so, at every chance I got, I was in my little closet office, fanny to the chair, deep in teaching preparation. My office really was a closet, but it was a huge closet with a window. I put a desk in there, a telephone, a lamp, and a little bookshelf. But all of my clothes were in there too. Josiah had a real office at the English department and a desk in our library. I could have had the library for my desk, but I liked my little nook with its window that looked onto our maple in the front yard.

On the Wednesday after the opera Sunday I was in there planning out the next day's lesson while James took his morning nap and Wallace was in day care. Josiah appeared in the door with his coat on and bag slung over his chest like a bike messenger. He looked fresh-faced and radiant.

"Bully? Hi. I am going to have lunch with Sylvia today to help her with her job applications," he said.

I was eye level with sleeves.

"Oh, great," I said, and stuck out my tongue. "Okay, just go have lunch with the beautiful and talented Sylvia. Don't worry about me, I'll just be cutting up bananas for James and eating grilled cheese."

"Oh, Bully. No, she asked me for help . . . please. No sharing," he said.

"No sharing" was something we said to each other a lot. Josiah cheated on his first wife and although I had completely explained that away, I still got nervous about it. "Once a cheater always a cheater" is something people say a lot, so in order to address the doubt full-on we had many talks about it. He never failed to make me feel better by saying he knew firsthand how destructive cheating was and he would never willingly do it again, especially because of Wallace and James. He came up with the phrase "No sharing." He would look me right in the eye and say, "No sharing." And then I would repeat it. No sharing. I had even told his stepmother that I was 100 percent sure that Josiah would never leave me. "Why?" she

said in her North Carolina accent. "Because we just don't think that is going to happen," I would say, brimming with self-confidence.

"Well, I wish I could come," I said, fake pouting.

"Me too. I'll be home at the usual time," he said. "I love you!" And he bounded down the stairs.

This turn of events was enough for me to shoot downstairs and call New York. I had left a handful of beloved friends in New York and, as much as I was trying to establish like friendships in Ohio, nothing would ever match these pals. The fact is I was on the phone with one of them daily.

So I called Lisa.

"Hey," I said, stepping outside onto the back deck.

"I'm having a paranoid thought and I want you to dispel it for me," I said, balancing on a rock.

"Okay," Lisa said. Lisa really should be a shrink. She is calm and Jewish and gives very levelheaded advice. We met because we lived across the street from each other in New York and our first kids had the same due dates. We were exactly alike. She was an actress; I was an actress. She was married; I was married. She had a sister-in-law who was a milliner; I had a sister-in-law who was a milliner. She had two cats, one of whom was named Nora; I had two cats, one of whom was named Nora. The only difference we could see was that she was Jewish and I was Episcopalian.

"Josiah went to the opera for too long with Sylvia on Sunday and now he is going to lunch with her to help her with her job applications," I said.

"Why did he go to the opera with her on Sunday?" she said.

"Well, I didn't want to go, so I said he should take her," I said.

"Hummm," she hummed.

"But that's not a big deal. Apparently it ran too long and it was a time-management disaster. I just don't like that they are having lunch. I don't like friends who are girls. I am nuts—right?" I said.

"You know, yes, you are. But I get it. Eric doesn't have friends that are girls on purpose. He doesn't even have girls working in his office, just so there's no confusion," she said. Now, that is going a little far, but there is a comfort to Eric's extreme position.

"I know. My father and brother really don't have any girl friends. I'm not sure you can have friends who are girls if you are married," I said.

"You have lots of friends who are men." I did.

"I know. You are right. I'm crazy. She is lucky he is helping her with her job applications. From what I can see she is useless at it," I said.

It was true. I had been kept up-to-date about Sylvia's job application process by Sylvia. She was only appointed the adjunct eighteenth-century job for one year. She had to do the job search again, but the thing was she was having a hard time doing it. She was not putting in the effort one must to deal with that nightmare. It was like she didn't want to go anywhere else. I couldn't blame her, but it did occur to me that since she had no choice in the matter she might need to at least try to get another job.

"Don't worry," Lisa said.

"You're right, I won't. I just don't like this feeling."

"Here's something interesting," she said. "Why do you think you told Josiah to take Sylvia to the opera?"

"I know," I said, catching her drift.

"Were you testing him?"

"I know—that's weird. But maybe I was testing myself? Or proving to myself that I'm cool and not jealous of this chick."

"Are you? Jealous of her."

"Well—no. Yes, a little, just because she is that small, dark-haired Winona Ryder type that I know he likes and I can never be," I said.

"Ugh—small girls, can't stand 'em," said all five feet ten inches of Lisa.

We got off the phone because I heard James waking up from his nap. His bedroom window faced the back lawn. Soon Grace would be there and I would be off to teach. It was Wednesday.

18

Our routine in the mornings almost never changed. Josiah would get up with the boys and let me sleep while he gave them breakfast. I was still nursing James and most nights was up with him at least two or three times. He was not nearly as good a sleeper as Wallace had been. (It is amazing how kids differ from one to the next. For instance, James is very particular about what he wears. "Noooo, I would like the socks with the red stripes, please, not the blue ones. I already have a blue shirt on, Mama." Where Wallace just pulls out whatever is on top, puts it on backward, and walks out the door.) Then, during *Sesame Street,* I would go downstairs and eat my breakfast while Josiah showered. I would bring the boys' clothes downstairs with me and get them dressed as Elmo bid everyone farewell until the next day. We would then all pile into the van (including Plover the dog—nobody likes being left behind) to drive Wallace to day care. Josiah would drive and sing funny songs to the boys. Josiah made up these really clever songs for each boy. The best was one he made up for Wallace about his being a Chinese emperor. Wallace looked like Puyi until he was about one. It went like this, to the tune of the theme song from *Empire of the Sun,* the Steven Spielberg movie:

"You are our little Chinese emperor. You are our little Chinese king. You have armies up in Hunan, you have castles in Beijing. You're surrounded by your regents, you look tiny on your throne. You are our little Chinese emperor. You are our little Chinese king."

Once Wallace was reasonably happy and settled in with Miss Marsha and Miss Sanya, I would take over the wheel and drive Josiah to the English department. We would wave good-bye to him until he was in the door, and then I drove James, Plover, and myself home to make beds and finish cleaning up the dishes from breakfast. We did this every day.

So on the next day, as we were driving down College Street to the day-care center, Josiah says, "So should I tell Sylvia that we are on for our regular Thursday dinner?"

"Yes, yes. It's the farm day so I think I'll make that chard and tomato tart. Should we also have a steak?" I said.

"Why not?" he said.

"Okay, you cook 'em, I'll buy 'em. I'll go to the IGA after I drop you off," I said.

I reveled in the domesticity and again had put aside what I was sure was only an insecure feeling on my part that somehow Josiah liked Sylvia. And even if he did have some affinity for her, she was married, we were married—and even if she was married to her pale, perfectly nice cousin whom she never spoke of, we were happily married, we had lots of great sex, even with two children and no nanny, and on top of that there was James sitting in his car seat in the back to prove it.

I dropped him off, turned the van around, and flitted off to the market to buy good Midwestern steaks for three.

I was able to go to the farm stand before it started to rain that afternoon. Big, heavy Ohio rain. I like crappy weather when I am having people over for dinner. It sets the mood of the evening and creates a need-to-be-inside-and-taken-care-of feeling. The chard and tomato tart I was making made me feel like I was Julia Child herself. It had Gruyère cheese in it, which makes it taste very French and sophisticated. It's really rather easy and if you have the privilege of using vegetables that you pick yourself from a nearby farm or your own garden, you will find nirvana in that little pie. I assembled it in the evening while the boys were eating their supper before Josiah came home. Pie shell, chard, tomato, cheese, chard, tomato, cheese, tomato, thyme, parmesan, and whack it in the oven. As the smell of the baking crust started to waft around the kitchen, Josiah came home to play with the boys and bathe them. I used the time to plump pillows and turn on the lights in the library. Although Sylvia had been over to our house countless times in the last month, I still wanted everything to look as calm and pretty as possible. I also wanted her to really get the picture of just how lovely the life going on inside this big brick house was.

Sylvia came over around 7:30 p.m. when the boys were well on their way to sleep. I opened a bottle of red wine for Sylvia and me—Josiah still wasn't drinking—and we sat in the kitchen around the island as Josiah cooked the steaks. I had set places at the island and put the tart and candles in the middle of the island. In retrospect, it's like I was cooking a romantic dinner for the two of them, which is nuts because at the time I felt like I was inviting her into our romantic dinner. Josiah and I always ate by candlelight, we always cooked for each other, I always had a glass of wine as we told each other our days. She was just getting a front-seat view of it. To me, she was seeing an example of what you can achieve if you put hard work into a marriage and keep your eye on the ball of your shared goals. We were showing her how it was done. That's what I thought I was doing, but as that particular night went on I found myself feeling like the third wheel. Once we started eating dinner it got worse. Sylvia would actually gaze into Josiah's eyes as he refilled her glass (forgetting to refill mine). She complimented him on his divine steaks and he blushed. I think I pathetically even got out our wedding album to point out someone we were talking about.

"Oh, Sylvia doesn't need to see that," he said.

It was confusing, and everything seemed to be going really fast. We got on the topic of having a friend of the opposite sex when you are married. I can't remember if I brought it up—and maybe because I was starting to really vibe something weird, I did, just to test it out.

"But of course you can have a friend of the opposite sex—how crazy to think anything else," Sylvia said.

"Well, I know that is the correct thinking, but really, is it always appropriate? Josiah and I talk about this. We feel differently about it," I said.

"Well, it would seem very insecure to me to say that your husband couldn't be friends with someone just because she is a woman," she said.

"Well, let's take Ward and Secca. I adore them both and feel that they are equally our friends. I would call Secca any day of the week to have lunch, but you would have to put a gun to my head to call Ward to have lunch," I said truthfully.

"That's sad," she said.

"I don't think so. I think it's just an unspoken rule that you should live by so that you don't get into any sticky situations where someone would feel uncomfortable. I care deeply about my marriage and never would want to put it in jeopardy."

"But your marriage surely would not be in jeopardy just because you had lunch with a friend, no?" She looked at Josiah.

"I am just old-fashioned, I guess," I said, feeling like a nerd.

"It's lovely," she said.

At this point I think Sylvia and I had finished the bottle of wine and Josiah had started clearing the dishes.

"It's getting late and I have to teach tomorrow," Sylvia said.

"You are right—I have all those *Spoon Rivers*, Josiah."

"Oh, do you teach on Fridays, Isabel?" she said.

(*What?* I thought. We all teach on Fridays. She knows that.)

"Yes."

And then I did another questionable move—it was becoming a trend.

"Josiah, darling, you will drive Sylvia home? It's raining cats and dogs out there."

"Of course. Don't do the dishes. It was a delicious tart."

And after hugs and thank-yous they went out the door into the rainy night. And, of course, I started doing the dishes.

19

On Friday it was still pouring. Everything was wet all day. The car was wet, my skin seemed wet, the dog was constantly wet. There was no escaping it. It was the first day my class was doing *Spoon River.* Spoon River is a fictional town and everyone in it is dead. The poems are the dead townspeople's soliloquies from the grave. Each character has something specific to say to the audience. Actors studying the Meisner technique do them as monologues. The point is to find out what the character is trying to say and to connect with the meaning behind it. Jealousy, rage, fear, remorse, guilt, happiness, bereavement. And so on. The question you want the students to answer is, What if? What if you were swindled out of all your money? What if your husband poisoned you? What if you lost an election unfairly? How would you feel? It takes a while for people to know how they feel about something. Being an actor is all about knowing very clearly how you feel about everything and then being able to live through those feelings on the stage or screen. When you watch Meryl Streep choose between her babies in *Sophie's Choice* you know very specifically how she feels about it. The thing is, in life we can't react truthfully to everything we feel. We build up important walls to block the feelings so we can behave like civilized people in society. What if we reacted truthfully to how we feel about pollution? We would be ranting lunatics on the streets of New York yelling at every driver for poisoning the air. But when you are acting, the challenge is to break down those protective walls and show people exactly how you feel about the circumstance you are in. If you feel it, the audience will.

Teaching *Spoon River* made me feel very alive and vulnerable. To open the students up I had to open myself up. Students are like audience members, not easily fooled. They have a finely tuned bullshit meter and they will use it every second that you are standing up there.

I was a live wire when I taught that Friday, and it didn't turn off so quickly after the class ended.

I ended class twenty minutes early. I had a sitter who was with the kids and although they loved her, the second I walked through the door, Mommy free time would be over. So I didn't want to go home. What I wanted was to have a cup of tea and talk more about *Spoon River.* Lucky for me, I thought, Josiah's office was in the building next to the theater building. I knew he was done with teaching and had a break until he had to go to a doctor's appointment that afternoon. Delighted at the thought of an unplanned tea with my husband, I ran through the pouring rain over to King, the English department. Josiah's office was on the second floor, which really felt like the first floor. The first floor was actually the basement. All the offices were along a wide hallway. The professors decorated their doors with stuff that made it clear what subject they taught. Postcards, quotes, office hours, boxes to put papers in. It really felt like college in there. It was cozy because you always saw someone you knew.

Josiah's office was halfway down the hall. He had put a batik cloth over the window on his door and over that behind the glass were poems and photographs of poets and lots of evidence that through the door you could find a poetry scholar.

I was wet and in a rush and had two bags, one for me and one for my teaching, and was hopeful that I would find him in there and he hadn't had his afternoon cup of tea yet. I did one of those knock-and-open things where if someone wasn't ready for you they would have no time to get ready. I opened the door and there they were. Josiah and Sylvia were sitting at his desk head-to-head with two cups of tea, sitting way too close.

"What is this!" I demanded.

"Sorry," Sylvia said. She stood up quickly and headed for the door.

"No. Stay. Really," I said, mad as hell and undone by what I had just interrupted.

"We are working on Sylvia's job search, Isabel." Josiah sounded pissed and short. Everything was spinning, and I didn't know what to do. I looked down and saw an unmailed bill I had asked Josiah to mail more than a week before.

"I'll just mail this!" I yelled at them and slammed the door.

What the fuck, I thought. What the fuck is going on?

Did I just see that? Did I make it up? Am I going crazy? I had run outside and was standing under the lip of the roof just out of the rain, but it was still splattering on me. I think I was crying. How could I go home? The kids were there. I couldn't go back in. Where could I go? There was nobody around; it was as if I was in a college ghost town and the only other five people in it were my husband and my friend Sylvia, who were huddled in his office, and my boys and their babysitter, who were making popcorn in my house. I ran to Too Chinoise and stood breathless and dripping in front of the cash register and Ben the waiter. Ben was the only guy in there as it was four o'clock. He knew me well. He knew my boys, so I thought I could just ask for a glass of water and sit on a chair by the door for a second. He didn't say anything as I sat in my wet coat and drank the water and wondered what turn my life had just taken.

20

When I got home the boys were in a sea of construction paper, glitter, and glue at the kitchen counter making fancy hats. Oberlin students take babysitting to the next level. The house smelled of popcorn and all the lights were on as it was getting darker earlier and earlier. It was a happy scene, so happy that I put the afternoon's drama to the side. I set about making myself very busy fixing the boys supper and waiting for Josiah to get home from the doctor. We were going out that night with the English department gang, including Sylvia, to a new Mexican restaurant that had just opened in town, and I had been looking forward to it. It was an event, something new. There would be margaritas involved and a big table of friends and too much food. I would make a good dinner for my boys, welcome my husband home, and then pass the boys over to him to play with while I went upstairs to take a bath and get pretty. Maybe he would not mention the scene in his office. I certainly wasn't going to. But he did.

He darted into the kitchen through the back door, getting out of the rain.

"My boys!" he said as he kicked the doormat with his boot, getting the mud off. Wallace beamed a smile full of carrots at him and James reached out of his high chair yelling, "Dada!" Confident that the warm house full of good smells and his boys would melt away any anger he had at me left over from earlier in the day or confusion that he might have about Sylvia, I walked over like June Cleaver and put my arms around his neck.

"My sweetheart, how was the doctor?" I said.

He stood stiff and when I let go he said under his breath, "What the fuck were you thinking today? You made Sylvia very upset."

The boys were two feet away from us. When people describe a room spinning after something unthinkable happens, like the death of a parent or news you have lost your job, it's because you have lost the context of your life and your eyes literally are looking for things to ground you, to remind you that you are still in your life. The room started spinning, but my eyes found the side of the counter. Josiah and I had spent hours deciding what shape the curve of the counter should have. There are many different grooves you can choose or you can have it quite plain. We chose to have one groove in the middle of the curve. Elegant and simple. I held on to the counter and felt the groove under my hand, reminding me that we had built this house. We had chosen colors and fixtures and a life and that was more, much more than this blip with fucking Sylvia.

"Are you kidding me?" I murmured. "What were you two doing? I felt like I walked into something."

"Well, you didn't. I am helping Sylvia with her job applications. You have got to get a hold of yourself," he said coldly.

He's right, I thought. Somehow I had gotten it wrong. I was paranoid and insecure. I instantly wanted to take all responsibility, apologize, and have it be over and have us go back to a time when he would have been happy to see me on a Friday night.

"I'm sorry," I whispered. "Please, can we forget it? I'm sorry."

He stood there and looked irritated. He made a move to get out of the kitchen, away from the boys, who were starting to be done with dinner and ask for Popsicles. "I'm going upstairs," he said.

"Why don't you let me go up? You haven't seen the boys and I'm cold and need a bath," I said.

He took a quick breath in. "Fine," he said. He looked at me with absolutely no pleasure. I had never seen that expression on his face before.

We kept our plans and went out with everyone that night. Sylvia showed up too. But right before we got out of the car to go in the restaurant I said, "This feels awkward. Maybe you should just go."

"It will be rude if you don't go now," he said.

"I don't think anyone will give a fuck if I'm there or not," I said, wanting him to differ with me.

"Well, make a decision because we are late," he said. Josiah hates to be late to anything and rarely is. Of course I didn't want to go home, so I got out of the car and watched him run in the rain ahead of me through the parking lot. I had never been in that parking lot, which was weird in such a small town. I didn't recognize where I was and I had never felt so alone.

My dreams of a fantastic new Mexican restaurant were soon dashed. The margaritas were made from a mix and the shrimp in my fajitas were the small kind that I think come out of a can. I had imagined us sitting around a round table that was lit with many candles, but instead it was a long table where the people on the end get left out of the conversation, and there was only overhead lighting. I seemed to be more concerned that the restaurant was disappointing than about the fact that there was suddenly a dangerous rip in my marriage. It didn't occur to me at all that the rip could get bigger. Josiah told me I had made a rash and unfair judgment and I was ashamed. But, I thought, I could make it better again.

Sylvia barely spoke to me that night. Well, I thought, I have made her uncomfortable. She probably was embarrassed at the insinuation I had made earlier. Josiah wasn't talking to me even though he was sitting next to me. He was angry at me. The service was terrible so this hellish dinner went on far longer than it had to. I was trying to get a buzz on to kill the unbearable awkwardness, but the margaritas were not at all strong so I just felt sick from all the syrup. Maybe sensing there was something bizarre going on at the table, Secca and Ward frantically overdescribed a farmers' market that they went to every Saturday in the parking lot of Trader Joe's right outside of Cleveland.

"Oh, let's all go tomorrow!" I said, thinking more time

together would be an answer. "The boys will love it. We have nothing to do tomorrow, do we, Josiah?"

"No," he said.

And so we made a plan to meet at our house at nine the next day, Secca, Ward, Sylvia, and us.

21

My heart felt worried. I felt I had done something wrong, but I also had this gut instinct that something was going on between Josiah and Sylvia. I saw it after all. Josiah was powerful to me, though. If he made a statement, I believed it. And he said I was wrong.

When I was living in Williamsburg, Brooklyn, the first year that we were together, he would drive down from Cambridge on Friday evening and I would have a big dinner ready for him in my little kitchen with a bathtub in it. He would bring big bunches of my favorite Casablanca lilies, we would make love, and then eat dinner by candlelight in the kitchen. One night I roasted an entire Arctic char fish with fennel. It was superb. The next day we had lunch with my parents and I bragged to my mother about my accomplishment.

"How did you figure out how to do that?" my mother said.

Without missing a beat, I recounted for her exactly how one roasts a whole fish. It's not hard at all to roast a fish, but there are certain things that she just doesn't do. Roasting a fish, or a chicken, almost, falls into the category of more trouble than it's worth. It's just how she is.

"Why does your mother not think you are capable of doing something as easy as roasting a fish?" Josiah said later.

"Oh, I think she just thinks it's hard."

"But she said, 'How did *you* do something like that.' She knows you can cook. I thought it was really undermining."

Yeah, I thought. Does my mother think I am such a loser I can't open a cookbook and follow directions? I had never thought about it before, but now that Josiah had highlighted it, it made all the sense in the world. He was my advocate, my defender against my mother, who thinks I am too lame to roast a fish. He said it and it was law to me.

I rarely questioned anything Josiah said. He felt smarter to me than most people I knew. When he said I was wrong about what I saw in the office, I believed him. Almost.

I felt like I was in the doghouse that Friday night. We got home and Josiah paid the babysitter and took the dog out for a walk. I checked on the boys and started getting ready for bed. I was in bed when Josiah came upstairs.

"That was a terrible night," I said.

"Yes, it was."

"Can't we make up? I'm sorry about today, but you have to admit it wouldn't be a fun thing to walk into if you were me. Can't you at least see how it would look suspicious?" (I could feel myself about to cry, but did everything not to. I cry a lot for good reason, but I also cry easily. So does my mother. Hymns in church, kids trying hard, I even cried watching *Tommy Boy* with Chris Farley.)

"Oh, Isabel," he said (he never called me Isabel), sounding weary and frustrated.

I was now sitting up on his side of the bed. I couldn't believe he wouldn't concede to my feeling that it was a strange thing to walk in on.

"You have always been overly jealous of all the women in my life who are just my friends. It's really a problem and I think you should talk to Dr. Bergen about it," he said.

Dr. Bergen was our couples therapist in New York. Josiah had a point, I thought. Dr. Bergen was a genius, classic Upper West Side shrink and probably would be able to get us out of this mess. In our New York City days we had seen her on and off when we would hit rough spots. There was one time, in our first year of living together on Seventy-second Street, when we were thinking of moving to Cambridge sort of on a whim. It was a bad idea at the time because there was so much going on—we were planning on getting married, I was on two TV shows, Josiah was writing his dissertation. We had good friends we saw all the time. But for some reason we were both obsessed with the theory that life would be better if we moved north. We were flirting with the idea of having a baby, so that was fueling our thinking. We were constantly writing lists of pros and cons—to move or not to move. It was plaguing us. In one session, Dr. Bergen just said, "Do you *have* to go to Cambridge?"

We looked at each other. "No," we said at the same time.

"Then don't," she said plainly. Oh my goodness, in that one sentence the entire weight of the world came off my shoulders. Josiah and I practically did a jig in her office and went to Krispy Kreme Doughnuts after and had two each, we were so relieved and happy. Not because we were staying in New York rather than moving to Boston, but because we had made a decision. Dr. Bergen tended to give you the answers.

But the fact was that we were far, far away from Dr. Bergen's office on 106th and West End Avenue, so I balked at Josiah's suggestion.

"Dr. Bergen? What are you talking about? Dr. Bergen is in New York and I am in Ohio, if you remember."

"Well then, someone else. But we are really in trouble if you are going to fly off the handle every time I am consulting with a colleague," he said in a very professional way.

"Sylvia isn't a colleague! She's my friend too and she was sitting too close to you!"

"In your warped view of things," he said loudly and sharply.

I put my head down and could feel myself about to sob.

"What the fuck, Josiah, why are you yelling at me? I am already so upset," I said, now crying.

"I don't know. I don't know," he said as he went into his closet to take off his shirt.

Then I summoned up some courage and decided to get a little dramatic about things just to see where they would go.

"Well, Josiah, if I am so fucking crazy and off the mark, swear on the boys that you are not in love with Sylvia!" I half shouted. I felt like I was in a movie when I said this. In the movies when the lady delivers an ultimatum like this, she usually gets the answer she wants. It felt slightly ludicrous, but I let it rip anyway. He whipped around so he was standing in the doorway of the closet and yelled, "This marriage is over!"

I sat silent. He went back into the closet.

"What on earth was that?" I said, as if someone had slapped me across the face. It seemed as if he was trying on some dramatic histrionics for size too. Did he really mean to say that?

"I just think that if you are going to make me avow on my children something like that, our marriage is in such a state of ruination, it is in perilous danger," he said with a withering formality.

And from that point on, Josiah started using very sophisticated vocabulary in our fights. I rarely understood him and would always ask for definitions.

I sat on the bed and cried hard. When he went into the bathroom, I followed him.

"You can't say that. You don't mean that," I said as he took out his toothbrush.

"I'm sorry, Isabel, but I do think what happened today says very bad things about where our marriage is." I sat on the side of the tub.

"You are an asshole," I said.

"If you are going to name call, this conversation is going to have to end," he said.

"But you are," I cried. "How dare you threaten me about our marriage!"

"Let's go to bed. It's late and you have been drinking," he said.

"Oh my God, I wish I was drunk," I said.

And then James started to cry and I had to go nurse him back down. By the time I got back to bed Josiah's light was off and he was asleep.

22

I woke up the next morning and for two seconds I didn't remember our fight from the night before. When I did it was like a little crash that took my breath away. I was alone in bed. Josiah had taken the boys down for breakfast. I didn't want to stay mad—I wasn't mad anymore, I was worried. I wanted so much for things to snap back and be okay. Our fights had been bad in the past, but we were able to recover and say no fighting and move on pretty quickly. I went into the kitchen, where they all were, and knew instantly things were not better. My heart sank when Josiah did not turn around when he heard me say hello to the boys.

We pushed through breakfast trying to protect the boys from what was going on, but how could Wallace not have picked up on the tension? Josiah did a lot of dishes with his back to us and I talked to the boys about the adventure we would be having at the farmers' market in Cleveland. It was like we were slipping down an icy hill. You think you are going to get control and stop, because how can a grown-up really slip down a hill? The ice can be more powerful than you and you might not have the right shoes. We were slipping, we were not getting our grip, and I couldn't believe it. I didn't believe it.

"Is Sylvia coming over here?" I asked.

"Yes, I believe everyone is meeting here so we can follow them," he said.

"Does she have to come in our car?" I said.

"No," he said.

Sylvia did come over. Wallace and James had just gotten some vitamins from the little health food store that looked and tasted like candy. When Sylvia knocked at the kitchen door, the boys went rushing to let her in and frantically waved the vitamins in her sight line. They made her eat two.

She talked to the children like someone who doesn't have children. She was self-conscious and overly polite. I would never have eaten those vitamins but she did because she was uncomfortable. Seeing this made me feel safe. She'd better feel uncomfortable looking at our children. If marriage wasn't something she valued, she must have some respect for the fact that two people had children, for Christ's sake. This was all going to blow over because the reality was that I was married to Josiah and those were our two children. I was married to him.

Sylvia went with Secca and Ward. We all got in different cars and headed out of our little town to Cleveland. In the car we were listening to a Dan Zanes album with a heartbreaking version of "Shenandoah." Dan Zanes has changed kids music from saccharine, yo-yo crap that an adult can barely stand listening to, to sophisticated, life-giving music that you never want to turn off. Lots of banjos and mandolins. That fall we listened to this one album endlessly. Even when it was clear we were not going to make it, Josiah and I still sang along to the words of "Shenandoah" together, driving in the car with our sons.

"I think you should apologize to Sylvia," said Josiah twenty minutes into the drive. This was the first thing he had said since we left the house.

"What should I say?" I said.

"Tell her that we were having time-management problems and that your outburst has nothing to do with her and you are sorry," he said.

I looked back at the boys, who were looking out the window at the farmland.

"Okay," I said. "But won't it be weird to bring the whole thing up again?"

"No, I think she feels very uncomfortable and you should take responsibility and apologize. I don't know that it will work, but it seems . . . I just feel badly that she is caught up in all our shit."

I didn't think we had any "shit" to get caught up in, and when did he talk to her about how uncomfortable she was? But I was desperate to get back in his good graces so I readied myself.

In the Trader Joe's outside of Cleveland they have these mini–shopping carts for kids to push around. Both Wallace and James wanted one to "shop" with and even though it was like turning puppies loose in a pet shop, I couldn't say no. For a while I hovered over them, keeping them from hauling down every cereal box and loaf of bread, but when I saw Sylvia in the dairy aisle, I abandoned them and set about my task of apologizing. Josiah was engrossed in the fine organic tea section, ignoring both of his wandering toddlers and his wife and "friend" next to the heavy cream. Sylvia's eyes widened as she saw me coming. Deep breath, I thought.

"Hey, I just wanted to say sorry about my freak-out yesterday. Josiah and I are having time-management problems. It had nothing to do with you," I said.

"Oh . . . umm . . ." She was mumbling and looking down at the chevre in her hand. "I am sorry—we were just working on my job stuff that I am impossibly behind on."

"Yeah . . . well, I shouldn't have blown up like that. I can be very impulsive. It's totally my fault," I said.

"Don't worry."

"Good. Where are you applying anyway?"

"Oh, I can't even think about it . . . I am so behind . . ." she said. She was so self-deprecating.

"Yeah, you should get on it, huh?" I said.

"Yes. I am very behind," she said.

I went to find Wallace and James, whose little carts were brimming with Boca Burgers and oranges. They looked at me with the proudest faces.

That night I had to go to a show produced by, directed by, and starring one of my students. She was a radical brunette lesbian who looked like the girl next door, but would shock me with all sorts of sophisticated lesbian talk about dental dams and fisting. The play was about cutting. I had never heard of cutting, which only shows that

I am a generation older than these students. It's like how our parents knew that some girls threw up after they ate but they had never heard of the word *bulimia* until it showed up and the school started talking about it. Cutting is what some adolescent kids do when they are depressed or feel alone. They take razors and cut their own skin. It makes them feel alive, or in control. It's one of those self-mutilation problems that is very troubling and worrisome and apparently exists all over America. I went to the play by myself and Josiah stayed at home with the boys.

The show was in a black-box theater called the Hole. Almost all of my class was in it. At first my students were very suspicious of this young TV chick coming in and making them cry and imagine their worst fears and greatest hopes, but they were warming to me. I could tell because the girls started asking me advice about their hair color and the boys teased me and called me the Gill-monster—which I've since learned is a hideous huge lizard. I think they used the term in a loving way, though. I really knew I was in with them when they invited me to professors' beers. There is a campus bar in the student center, and on Thursdays at five, professors can be invited by their students to buy beer for their class and drink it with them. It's a great honor.

I was relieved to get away from our house and the boys and Josiah, who for the rest of the day after we got home from the farmers' market was almost silent and so distant I wished he would just go to the office, which he finally did for a couple of hours before I had to leave for the show.

The show was mostly testimonials about cutting read

by the students who were all dressed in black. It was heavy and sad. Who knew that all these children had it so bad they would spend hours making hairline incisions in their own skin. I thought of my boys and hoped that they would not have to go through such an awful twist of growing up, but mostly I thought about Josiah. Was Josiah somehow depressed and doing his own version of cutting by playing with the fire of an affair with Sylvia? Had I not understood some very real part of him that needed to be recognized? Was he injuring something as precious as his family to make me notice? These teenagers were calling out for attention and love. Was Josiah? Had I missed something? It seemed possible. I knew he was a dark guy, but did I ever let him express it? Did I suffocate him? Was I controlling like a parent, not letting him have the friends he wanted? It all started to make lots of sense. Marriages go through hard times because of miscommunication, but they can be fixed. Maybe it took this play to make me see the light. Maybe Josiah had always been misunderstood because he looks like one thing and inside is like another. I saw my chance to prove to him that I finally did understand that his insides needed to be acknowledged, that he didn't need to cut himself or me to get the attention he needed. I would accept him.

I said my congratulations to the cast and ran home. It was dark on the paths and the air was sharp with cold, but I ran faster. When I got home I ran upstairs in my coat. Josiah was a lump on his side of the bed. He had left the light on my bedside table on.

"Bully," I whispered.

He opened his eyes, but didn't sit up.

"How was the night?" I said.

"Fine. The boys were fine. James woke up once."

"Bully, the play was about cutters and it made me think a lot. Were you ever a cutter?" I said.

"No," he said.

"Well, anyway—that's good, but I was thinking. Maybe I haven't been so open to you . . . do you know what I mean?" I said.

He didn't respond.

"I mean, I want to know you and accept you and love every part of you," I said.

He didn't say anything.

"This play, it was awful. I mean it was good, but it was sad about these kids who feel trapped in some world they don't relate to so they cut their arms. It just made me think that everyone—humans—goes through so much in this life and feels so alone sometimes. We will be all right. I'm sorry that we have been in such a weird place. But people go through terrible times in their lives, like when they are cutters, and can come out the other side. We can. I love you," I said. I was stroking his hair.

"Bully, I am so tired. I'm glad you saw the play, but can we talk about this tomorrow?" he said.

"Okay, okay," I said.

I felt hopeful. We would get through this. I took a bath and went to sleep.

23

During the night I was up with James. Josiah let me sleep the next morning. It was Sunday. Ominous Sundays, but I woke up feeling like this might be a more normal day. I could hear the boys watching TV in the living room and I could smell waffles that they must have just finished. I walked down the stairs, and when I was almost at the bottom I saw Josiah sitting in the library on a rocking chair I had given him. It was a very low and small chair. My mother and I had bought the chair at an auction in Maine. I had covered it in a Gillies tartan that a friend had given me in my early twenties after he returned from a trip to Scotland.

Josiah was sitting on the chair with his head in his hands. Everything went still but for the sound of *Sesame Street* coming from the other room. I went into the library and knelt in front of him. He looked up at me and tears streamed out of his eyes. His mouth crumpled downward and he squeezed his eyes shut. He put his head down again, this time almost at his knees, and started

sobbing uncontrollably. He was shaking and heaving sobs. I knew this cry. This was the cry of someone whose heart was breaking.

"No, no, no. No, Bully. Whatever this is, stop it," I said.

He cried even harder.

"Please, baby. Don't go where you are going. Stop—we will be all right. Please, Josiah."

"Nooo," he groaned. "No, we won't." He could barely get the words out. "We won't. I can't do it. I can't do it."

"What? What can't you do?" I said. I was crying now.

"I can't do it. I can't do it. I can't," he cried.

"Yes you can. Baby, please. Stop," I said.

But he was gone. I knew he was. He was leaving me and I knew from the way he was crying that he wasn't going to come back. He had crossed a line and I was on the other side of it. He had decided and it broke his heart. It was October 6. I will never see him again, I thought. In those five minutes I lost my husband. I knew it as clearly as I did when I found him at the foggy wedding in Maine.

Part Two

Bully

24

The sound of the PBS music announcing that *Sesame Street* was over snapped me out of what was happening in the library with Josiah. I walked in to see the boys.

Stunned. Stunned. I was really stunned and at a loss as to what to do or where to look. I was sure of one thing: I had to get the kids away from me. I was like an arm that had just been cut but had not yet begun to bleed. If I could get the children out of the house before I started to bleed I'd be all right. Josiah was already dressed. He could drive the boys somewhere. I was in my nightgown and couldn't.

"Take the boys to Carlyle," I said. He nodded and started getting the boys ready. I helped him and went through the motions of finding socks and boots and sweaters. I filled up sippy cups with juice and put string cheese in Baggies.

"Take the dog too," I said. If he could have taken the cats I would have asked him to. I needed to be alone. I didn't want any living creature around me.

"She'll get cold in the car," Josiah said.

"It's not that cold. Just take the dog," I said.

The boys wanted me to go, but I couldn't. I couldn't get in the car. It wasn't like any other day. Everything felt different and I had been awake for only thirty minutes. I suddenly didn't feel married to Josiah. How can that be? How could this be happening?

Boys in car seats. Josiah in the front seat with the dog. He looked at me, pressed his lips together, and nodded. Like he was the milkman making his way down the block.

I headed back into the house still in my nightgown.

What is happening, what is happening? I was chanting that phrase in my head. It was steady and had no emotion yet. Those words were the only thing I could think.

"Having some 'me' time?" It was my dance professor neighbor, Randall, who had just seen the kids and Josiah drive away in the car.

"Josiah is leaving me!" I wanted to shout back. But I didn't. I just smiled and nodded and gave him the thumbs-up.

Inside, the kitchen was warm, but a mess. I started clearing the plates and putting away the orange juice.

What is happening, what is happening?

I loaded the dishwasher, wiped down our counters, straightened the chairs, refilled the water in the vase of flowers on the island.

What is happening, what is happening?

I made tea in the tea-making place. Josiah had set up a part of the counter that had everything you would need to make a cup or pot of tea at any time of day. He dutifully refilled the sugar in the sugar bowl, stocked the tea, and made sure all the mugs and cups were in easy reach. It was like a mini-Starbucks.

I carried the tea upstairs and let it cool while I took a shower. *What is happening, what is happening?*

I got dressed in jeans and a long-sleeved T-shirt, sat on the side of the unmade bed and brushed my hair, made the bed, and took my tea downstairs to the library.

What is happening, what is happening?

25

I sat at the big desk that had been in the library of the house where Josiah grew up in Florida, and looked at the 8 × 10 framed picture of Josiah and me on a beach with his son Ian. Until four weeks ago, when Josiah hung all the pictures all over the bathroom, this had been the only framed picture in the house.

As I looked at it I still felt nothing. I was not bleeding—yet. This was when I picked up the phone and called Bess. Bess is my best and oldest friend. She's the sister, she is my movie-in-the-middle-of-the-day pal, she is who I think of first. We are the godmother to each other's children. She lived in New York with her husband and, at that point, two children, one of whom was a few months younger than James. I was about to shock the shit out of her. I knew she was upstate with her parents for the weekend. Her mother, Bea, would know something was wrong from the second she heard my voice. I dialed.

"Hellooo." Bea sounds like she is yodeling when she answers the phone.

"Aunt Bea Bea," I said, and started to tear up. The bleeding part was about to start.

"Izzle? What's the matter?" she said.

"Umm. I don't know, but I think I have to talk to Bess," I said.

"Okay, hold on, she's in the chicken coop with Blix. Hold on. Hold on," she said lovingly. I think people know right away when something is really wrong. We are animals after all.

Aunt Bea Bea put down the phone and I heard her telling Bess's father to get Bess. I sat on the line and looked out the window at the dance professors, Randall and his wife, Tracy, loading into their car to go somewhere.

"Izzle?" Bess already sounded worried.

And then I bled. I took a big breath, opened my mouth, and cried out. I cried and cried. I couldn't make words. I was sucking in air and coughing it out. My whole face and the top of my T-shirt were drenched. I put my head down on the desk and wept into the phone.

"What is it! The boys? What has happened?" she said. She was so alarmed.

"Josiah is leaving me." I cried, and kept crying.

"What? No. Izzle, Izzle, don't worry. It's a big fight. Josiah would never leave you. Don't worry, don't worry. It's a fight," she calmed.

"No. No. He is. This is different. He is leaving me. He told me as much," I said, still out of control.

"What happened?" she said.

"There's been this weird thing all week with that girl Sylvia," I said.

"Your new pal?" she said.

"Yes, but I don't know. Something is happening—I can't explain it, and we got in a fight and it won't stop and I don't get it, but he is going to leave me, Bess, I know he is. He keeps saying, 'I can't, I can't . . .'" I sobbed.

"Where is he?" she said.

"With the boys at the nature place. He just left," I said.

"Don't you worry. It's just a fight. Fights can be big," she said.

"Bess, this is something different. I don't know why, but I know. I saw him sitting on a chair crying this morning and when I went to him to stop him or comfort him, I could tell in his eyes. He had left me. It's like he had just gone away." I started to cry again.

"Oh, my Izzle. Do you have tea?"

"Yes. But it's cold."

I thought, I had to call my parents.

"Bess, I have to call my parents," I said.

"Okay. I'm here. I'm here all day."

"I love you, Bess."

"I love you too, Izzle. Everything is going to be okay."

"Okay," I said like a five-year-old girl. And we hung up.

Now I thought of my parents. Did I want to bust this open? Would it make it more real? What if I told them and then Josiah came back and said he was just kidding and everything was fine? But that was not going to happen, I thought, because this felt deep. This felt like the real deal. This was the shit hitting the fan. I felt like you know when you know. I picked up the phone and called the apartment in New York.

My parents have lived in the same apartment all my life.

I was brought home from the hospital to it. It was a classic Upper West Side apartment on Central Park West. The windows in the living room and master bedroom looked right out over the park onto the reservoir and beyond that to Fifth Avenue. It was a marvelous apartment. I could imagine everything that was going on there as I sat at the desk in the library. My mother would just be back from the markets and getting ready to make my father lunch, which they would eat in the living room. Since it was a Sunday they might split a beer with their soup and sandwich. It would be sunny in the living room and my father would be reading the paper in his love seat. The Maine Coon cat, Arlo, would be next to him. I could feel the calm. I felt like I was in a fighter jet flying to the destination where I would drop a megabomb on an unsuspecting town, ruining people's lives for all eternity.

I dialed the number and waited.

"Hellooo?" My mother also sounded a bit like she was yodeling.

"Hi, Mumma," I said, still sounding like a five-year-old. I really couldn't think how I was going to say this.

"Good morning, Lula! Daaaaaaaddddaaaaa, it's Isheeee," she called. "Hold on, sweetheart, Dad's coming," she said. They always have to be on the phone together if ever a child calls.

I waited.

"Hi, Lula!" Dad said cheerfully. He is always cheerful.

"Hi," I said again, sounding meek.

I took a deep breath and thought, I'm not going to cry, but then I started crying. Not quite as raw as when I was on the phone with Bess.

"I think Josiah is leaving me. There is something going on and I don't really know what is happening, but I think he is leaving me and the boys." I shocked myself when I included the boys, and started sobbing into the phone.

My mother was silent. "Well then, you will take the boys and come home and live with us," my father said without missing a beat. He said it like he had known what I was going to say.

"Ishel, what happened?" My mother sounded tender.

"I don't know . . . Wait—Dad, I . . ." I wanted to say that his offer would be unnecessary. We couldn't really break up. Me moving to New York City with the boys by myself? It sounded crazy. But then I thought, yes, we could break up and I would have to live somewhere, and the only place I have to go is my parents'. But it was too much and I just started to cry again.

"Okay, Jesus. Lula, let's take a step back. Where are the boys?" Dad said.

"With Josiah at the nature place," I said.

I was thinking that there was nothing they could do now and I just better get off the phone.

"You guys? I think I should calm down. Maybe this isn't as bad as I think it is . . . It's been a shitty weekend. I'll wait and see how the day goes and call you later, okay? I just wanted to tell you because I just wanted to tell you," I said.

"Oh, my poor baby," my mother said. "It's Sunday. Have you had a bath? Do you have a cup of tea?" Her two antidotes to the blues and all else. I could feel her worry.

"Yes. I'll call you later."

And then we hung up. I could imagine what they

looked like when they met in the living room two seconds after they got off their respective phones. God, this was a nightmare.

I sat there, and even though there was hysteria in the air, I could also sense a pure and clear feeling of disappointment in myself. I have always had this beautiful example of a marriage to look up to. My parents are in love. They get it wrong sometimes and have what they would call a "Mr. and Mrs." (a strong disagreement), but they are encouraging of each other and respectful and kind most of the time. I had failed to make that happen in my own marriage. My husband was leaving me and whether he was doing that unilaterally or if I had everything to do with it, or it was both of us, he was leaving me, and I wasn't going to have a marriage like my parents', something I had wanted since I was a little girl. It was just so disappointing.

26

Josiah must have given the boys lunch on the road because when they got home it was their nap time. Thank God, I thought. So far I was handling this as if I were being broken up with by a boyfriend and I had no children. Every time I thought about being a mother as well, something went blank and I couldn't think anymore. Josiah and I put the kids to bed. James was already sleeping when I brought him to his nursing chair. He looked like a cherub with ketchup on his cheeks. I put my finger through the little curl under his ear and held on to him. Nobody could leave James, I thought. I put him in his crib, and as I closed the door I heard him sigh a big sigh like he was about to really go to sleep. I hoped he would sleep for four hours. Josiah was reading *Horton Hears a Who!* to Wallace in his bed. Wallace sucked his thumb and looked like he was going to fall asleep. Good. I wished I could fall asleep. I wished we could all fall asleep for one hundred years like in *Sleeping Beauty* when the entire kingdom falls asleep until the prince comes and kisses Sleeping Beauty in her tower. What if the entire town of Oberlin fell asleep and woke up when Josiah came to his senses and kissed me?

I waited for Josiah to leave Wallace's room and followed him downstairs. He headed straight for the tea place as if it were a bar. I sat on the window seat.

"Bully," I said. "Bully."

He was facing away from me. Maybe the drive with the boys changed his mind. Maybe it snapped him out of it.

"Do you want a cup of tea?" he said. Good sign, I thought.

"Yes, please," I said. "Bully?" I repeated.

"Isabel, I don't think we should call each other Bully anymore," he said.

I started to cry.

"Hey—listen, I'm sorry, but I just don't think it makes sense to call each other that," he said.

How do you just say, "I don't think we can call each other the name we have spoken every four seconds for the last six years"?

"Do you hate me?" I said. "Because you are killing me." I looked at him, hoping my tears would melt him. But he had the same look in his eyes that he had in the rocking chair. It was like he didn't know me. I felt like slapping him out of it. Where was he? We stared at each other. Every once in a while he took in little short breaths three times in a row. Like he was trying to fill his lungs with air. We were both panicking.

"I am going to the office," he said.

"It's Sunday," I said.

"I need to go for a few hours."

"The boys will wake up."

I felt like a teenager, and most teenagers I know don't have two children.

"I have been with them all morning," he said.

"But it's Sunday," I said again. This was so weird. Why were we talking about our boys like they were a football that we passed to each other? Maybe if I reminded him of his life he wouldn't walk out the door. It's Sunday and no matter how much I hated them, Sundays were family days and you got to spend them together until the bitter end when you went to bed. We did it every weekend. He didn't seem to remember his life.

Josiah filled his canvas bag with his computer and a few poetry books and walked out the door, leaving his tea steeping on the counter.

I was standing in my big new house with my boys asleep upstairs. My boys, I thought. I am alone with my boys and Josiah has just walked out the door. As I heard the front door rattle shut I turned from the teenage girl getting her heart broken into a mother again. I went upstairs to where the boys were sleeping in their rooms and sat in the hallway equidistant between them. I took in a long, steady deep breath, and when I couldn't take in any more, I held it. I think I held my breath for the next two months.

27

From that Sunday in early October until December 13, my life divided into three categories. The first was a continuation of the life we had started: children, teaching, house, and community in Oberlin. The second was managing to live with my husband, the father of my children, who had fallen out of love with me. And the third was trying to find out if he was having an affair with Sylvia.

Our families quite quickly got involved. Friends from New York and farther away were dumbfounded, but at the ready. I remember one friend of ours heard through another at a dinner party and dismissed the entire concept as a bad, ill-informed rumor. "I'm sure Josiah and Isabel are fine, how sick to say anything else." We were getting lots of how-can-this-be-true calls. We were seen by many, not all, I have since heard, as the perfect couple.

My father wrote Josiah a rather sharp email that Josiah showed to me, saying it was monstrous to refuse to work on the marriage, that something must be very wrong with him mentally. I was surprised at the harsh tone of the email. My father handles everything from higher ground than most people, takes all sides into consideration, uses diplomacy—he's famous for it in my world. He is a leader and he's wise. There are the few times, however, when he steps it up. If he feels there has been an injustice he can come down very hard. Josiah's mother came to her son's defense, taking issue with the word *monstrous.* I was a mother after all, so I could understand the parents aligning themselves, even if it was misguided, with their children. The email, and for that matter most of the details of our trouble, was being passed around. I was feeling torn in a zillion directions, agreeing and disagreeing with everyone at the same time. At one point Josiah, after seriously addressing my father's accusation, tried to lighten things by responding to the "monstrous" email exchange, saying couldn't we just blame the entire thing on my parents' cat, Arlo. It was classic Josiah to be able to make a fairly amusing joke during the worst crisis of our lives together. That's the thing, every once in a while he could make me laugh at our terrible state of affairs, while being the one that, I felt, was causing them. It was all very confusing and chaotic. And unlike Hurricane Katrina, which was unfolding more disastrously every day, this mess we had made ourselves.

28

In the movies when husbands or wives suddenly announce that they are leaving the marriage, life seems to stop suddenly to make room for the utter shit-storm that follows. The jilted woman or man has endless time to wallow in bed for days, crying or drinking. That actress never gets out of her nightgown, except to take long meaningful walks through Central Park. I needed to be in that movie. In my real life in Ohio absolutely nothing stopped. The mailman kept coming, I needed to go to work, the children still had to be taken to school and fed and washed and played with and loved. You were still invited to dinner parties, the phone rang off the hook, the laundry still spilled out of the hamper. If anything, your life became much, much, much busier because suddenly you had to deal with at least fifty family members and friends frantically trying to find out what happened and talk about what a disaster it all is. The circling wagons and campfires were inevitable and helpful, but they were time consuming, especially for someone who didn't have a nanny.

Running that house was no small feat. It had two floors, four bedrooms, a library, living room, dining room, kitchen, basement, and four porches. We had put in new appliances, a heating system, and electricity, but the house was 120 years old. It had its issues, and it had four people and three animals living in it. Being that it was the fall, every leaf on every one of our gargantuan old trees was about to drift onto the lawns that surrounded the house. That was another thing I didn't get about living in the suburbs. There are lawns. Lawns need to be cut, not once a month but once a week! And raking the *thousands* of leaves is grueling work that doesn't stop until it snows, and that's another nightmare that I won't even go into now, but think snow shovels.

I suppose that when your husband decides to leave you and your two children, everyone understands why your house turns into a shithole and your children walk around in dirty pajamas for three months. Nobody would expect you to produce a meal or hang a picture. You are given a free pass to be a mess in every way. But I didn't want that pass.

Maybe it's because I am my mother's daughter, and a stiff upper lip is the way my parents deal with disaster. Or maybe I was just denying everything. But I was not going to let my beautiful house fall apart or my children miss a birthday party because my marriage was circling the drain. Maybe I should have. Maybe I should have given in and let it all hang out, but how could I? There were beds to be made, and art drawers to organize. I had never been as busy in my life. Whether it was a bat in the attic or a conked-out lightbulb in the library, there was always something to clean or fix or deal with. It felt futile because in the back of my mind I knew very well that Josiah not wanting our life meant that we would have to sell the house. But I loved it. It gave me the greatest pleasure to oil the old oak banister or put pots of mums on either side of the front door. It was a real home and I wanted to treat it like one no matter what was going on.

29

Our family and house life didn't jive with the husband-having-his-own-life thing. The two realities kept smashing into each other. There was a dinner at the environmental building honoring Josiah's old advisor from Harvard, Helen Vendler, the poetry scholar. She is an academic giant and gave a series of lectures at Oberlin over the course of a week in October.

"So, I guess I'm not going tonight, huh?" I said to Josiah, who was making a peanut butter sandwich to eat at the office for lunch. Breakfast time was beginning to be one of the few times we saw each other.

"I guess not," he said quietly, carefully wrapping his sandwich in wax paper. I think he ate four hundred peanut butter sandwiches in the time I was married to him.

It was really awkward that we were having this conversation. Not a month before he had told me to get a babysitter for the evening. It was a big deal that Helen was in town. He respected this woman the way a chief of staff respects the president. I had never met her, although we had spoken on the phone many times. She gave both boys framed poems when they were born.

It felt like the entire town was going to this thing except for me. Certainly the entire English department would be there. I thought that it would stand out that I wasn't there and that felt embarrassing. It was at those kinds of events that I would feel the most proud of Josiah. It's cool to see your husband in his element, and dinners for poetry scholars were really his element. And the thing was, most other English professors look like what you would imagine—scruffy, thinning hair, awkward. But Josiah looked like the captain of the lacrosse team or a male model. People *did* confuse him for a model.

It was just funny that Josiah was so good-looking and a nerdy English geek all in one. He was like Indiana Jones. I always imagined that his students (male and female) might write "I love you" on their eyelids and bat them at him during his class.

Josiah went to the dinner by himself and while the boys slept I ate take-out Chinese food and watched horrifyingly stupid reality shows on MTV that at the time I found fascinating. Reality TV. Katrina. Angelina Jolie's relationship with the married Brad Pitt. The lady on E! kept saying things like "Representatives from both stars categorically deny the rumors." I would yell at the TV, "Bullshit! Of course they are in love!" I never thought I would feel such a strong bond with Jennifer Aniston. I had just settled into one of those shows when I heard a gushing sound from the kitchen. I ran in and there was a geyser of dishwashing water spouting from the dishwasher, which I had just turned on. As the water started to get out of control all over our new Brazilian almond floors, it dawned on me that I lived in a house in the country that I owned. There was no super downstairs to come to my rescue. I had zero idea what to do and had scooped up the dog so she didn't drink any of the soapy water. Panicking, I pushed every button on the machine to get it to stop, which it didn't.

Fuck fuck fuck! I thought. The boys were sleeping, I was sure of that, and the environmental building was just down the road. I ditched Plover and took off out the side door. I left the boys alone with the waters rising. What if the water caused an electrical fire? What if they woke up and went downstairs and drowned because the water had risen so high? What if they woke up and nobody was there? Why the fuck was Josiah at a dinner without me? Why do we live in a house with no super downstairs to call? Why is our brand-new dishwasher broken?

The dinner was being given on the first floor of the building, which is made entirely of glass (solar energy—get it?). As I booked up the street in my moccasin slippers, I could see the English department and all the college elders and special guests seated at round tables with maroon tablecloths. I searched for Josiah. Maybe he would see me through the window and I could signal for him to come, but truthfully I wanted to make the splashy, desperate entrance that the situation deserved so he and everybody we knew could see that leaving a wife alone with children in a big old house wasn't a good idea. By that point I had told some people that we were having troubles in our marriage. It's a terrible thing to have to admit to and it causes the life-in-a-fishbowl thing to go into high gear.

I pulled open the huge glass door, causing everyone to look over. My hysteria must have showed on the outside too, or maybe people just felt sorry for me from what they were hearing through the grapevine, because I got lots of looks as if I were a dog in the pound that nobody was adopting. I searched the room for Josiah and saw him sitting at a table next to Sylvia. He was deep in conversation with her as usual.

"Josiah," I gasped, and gave Sylvia a death glare.

"What happened?" he said, worried it might be the boys.

"The fucking dishwasher is exploding and the boys are alone in the house. You have to come home," I said, and gave Sylvia another pointed look—*See, I'm the wife with the kids and dishwasher. I'm the wife, I'M THE WIFE!*

He went with me. We both ran down the middle of the road home.

"Why is it every time I see you, you are sitting next to Sylvia?" I said while running.

"Oh, Jesus, Isabel. Can we focus on the matter at hand?" he said, and ran ahead to turn off the dishwasher. He could always find the button I couldn't find.

30

Unlike lots of men, Josiah didn't prolong the task of severing himself from me romantically. From that Sunday in our library on he never wavered in his conviction that he could not be in the marriage anymore. He never held my hand again, never touched me by accident as he rounded a corner in the kitchen, never gave me a wink, bought me a flower, called me a nickname. He never kissed me again, he never made love to me again. He never even looked at me lovingly again. Sometimes he would look at me in a worried way, and then he would look away.

He didn't want to be hurting me so badly, but he couldn't stop whatever had taken hold of him. I was out. It was so shocking to have all this happen in such a short amount of time but it made things extremely clear. Even the day before the library day I couldn't see him differently than I saw myself. We were all muddled up in each other, attached, entwined. I had no perspective looking at him. No objectivity. But now he had demanded a distance and from that distance I could see his behavior very clearly.

I also could see his behavior up close and personal because we were *living* together. In one day I went from living with my partner doing husbandy things to living with a teenager who was head-over-heels in love, but not with me. I can tell when someone is in love, even a stranger. It must be that the first flush of love gives off a pheromone or smell. It's in their smile, the way they breathe. People don't eat when they are in love, but people don't eat when they are divorcing either, so I don't know what that means. Love changes chemistry and you can just tell when it's happening, especially to your husband. The maddening and absurdly confusing part was that he was denying it. This was when I went into detective mode. He had brought most of his things to his office, so I searched for clues in his behavior. It was also the time when I ceased to sleep.

In driving school they teach you about total stopping distance time. You can't just stop a car short. Well, I guess you can, but you end up smashing your head and everybody else's head in the car. Josiah probably wished he could just slam on the brakes as hard as he could and get the fuck out of the car, but that would have killed the rest of us and he didn't want to do that. He had to slow the car down at a reasonable pace so we didn't slam into the car in front of us. But two months is an awfully small amount of time to slow down a family of four that has been together in one form or another for seven years. So it turned out that all of us ended up getting our heads slammed anyway.

One of the first parts of our life that had to be dismantled was our sleeping arrangements. I simply could not sleep. When Josiah said he couldn't be in the marriage anymore, I instantly lost that part of the human condition, the ability to fall asleep.

I have great parents, way above average, I would say. Like all people we don't always see eye-to-eye, and it is a parent-child relationship so it has had its complications, but generally I lucked out. And beyond my basic luck, my mother had had about ten really stellar moments. They are knockout moments that should go down in the parenting hall of fame. When I was a teenager, I had a college tour of California that was also a speaking tour for my father, who was running a lefty political think tank. During the day we would go see places like UC Santa Cruz, and at night he would lecture about post-Reagan America. As it happened, the Grateful Dead were also playing in California, and in an amazing display of coolness, my father let me go to a weekend of shows in Ventura while he watched the Celtics-Lakers play-off game at the Santa Barbara Biltmore. Lots of my pals were going to be there, but I had no idea where they were or where I was going to stay, but my dad let me go. This was in the days of no cell phones, so for a father to let his seventeen-year-old daughter join the masses of Deadheads walking toward the stadium to find her way for twenty-four hours was pretty amazing. He trusted me and he was right to because all I did was dance to "Sugar Magnolia" and sit around a beachy parking lot with a bunch of kids from Brown. I don't think I even had a beer. But I did meet and develop a crush on this blond, slightly sad hippie kid named Roberto. We wandered around the parking lot together mostly talking about music and drawing. We might have made out in the show, but it was pretty innocent. When I had to leave him to go find my father in Santa Barbara, he gave me this little green jade frog. That frog, I believed, led to bad luck for the next week. Little bad luck, like missing buses and ordering badly at restaurants, but I was convinced it was because of the frog. My dad and I went directly from our college/speaking tour to Maine, where my mother and brother Andrew were. Almost as soon as we got to the island I took my frog to my mother and told her my worry. When I think back on what I must have looked like then I sort of have to laugh. I was working the whole hippie thing. My hair was very blond and long. I wore long, beady earrings and many, many silver rings on my fingers. I had faded tie-dyes and ripped jeans. I just must have looked like a sweet cliché of every teenager in the world. Anyway, I went to her, very seriously, with my problem.

"Mum, I think this frog is bringing me bad luck," I said. She held out her hand flat for me to put the frog on and gave it a good look.

"Where did you get him?" she said.

"This boy Roberto gave it to me," I said, and I explained briefly what had gone on.

"Huh—well, if you really think this frog is bringing you bad luck, take him to the dock, say a proper good-bye to him, and toss him in the sea."

It made all the sense in the world to her what this frog was to me, nothing huge, but not meaningless. She didn't give me shit about who the feckless boy named Roberto was, she didn't blow me off, she just gave me good advice. Which I took. I took the frog from her, went around the house, marched to the water, and walked down the dock to its edge.

"Good-bye, frog. I hope the sea washes away your bad vibes and you find somebody else," I whispered.

Then I kissed it and threw it in the drink.

Years later when my mother found herself with the same girl having really bad luck in Ohio, she sent me sleeping pills so I could get through the day. It may sound trite, but I was blown over that she even knew what a sleeping pill was, much less that she had access to the stuff. I had heard both my mother and mother-in-law talk about not being able to sleep all the way through the night, I think it's a menopause thing, but there she was having a prescription for Ambien and no judgment about the fact that I needed it. She sent me four of them, and she instructed me to split each into three doses. I think the pills were ten milligrams each, so what I was taking was only three milligrams, about enough for an ant, but it did the job and I was beyond grateful for them. I ended up taking Ambien every night for the next six months. I often credit Paul Simon and Nora Ephron for getting me through my divorce, but right up on top of the list would also have to be the sleeping drug Ambien. I simply could not have done what I did without it. I should write the company a letter. You can't save your life and be exhausted at the same time.

31

As I am describing how things were eroding and being taken apart, it might sound very mechanical, ruthless, and cold, but that's how it felt. I believe it was because of the kids. I knew that our marriage was imploding, but I didn't want to let Wallace and James in on it, partially in hopes that I could turn it around, but mostly to protect them. I had to be precise and careful and mathematical and calculating and reasonable on the outside. I had to help Josiah rip away but not actually let it rip. Rips are messy, rips can make noise, rips are noticeable, I told myself. I had to be a surgeon, I told myself, help make a scar that would eventually heal so you could barely see it. I knew with everything in my body that careful, considerate moves were the way to save my fine, beautiful, sweet boys from this terrible misfortune that had befallen them. But inside, inside I was Pompeii. Inside it was as if a giant had reached down my neck, had taken hold of my insides and was squeezing and squeezing. My heart felt like it weighed thirty pounds. I held my tears back every second of every day. If they did come out, it was when I was talking to friends on the phone. The only place I felt comfortable allowing them out was the shower. I would crouch on my hands and knees, water falling and tears pouring out, wailing and heaving. My beloved husband whom I was so deeply in love with was going away from me and I couldn't stop him. Our children couldn't stop him. Our house couldn't stop him. Reason couldn't stop him. Money couldn't stop him. Our parents couldn't stop him. Nothing could stop him, and it made me want to tear my hair out and cry until the world itself ended. But the world wasn't going to end. In fact, it kept going at an alarmingly fast pace.

On the outside there was shit to deal with. We couldn't continue to sleep in the same bed. It was torture. At night I would long to have him hold me. I would pray that his foot would accidentally bump into mine and that he would keep it there. I had to exert every bit of energy not to reach out and touch his hair. He never did accidentally touch my foot. He never did turn to me to hold me. He fell asleep instantly with his back to me. It was agonizing, so we decided that he would move into the guest room with the beautiful orange grove William Morris wallpaper. He would sleep there until the early morning and then go to the boys before they discovered on their own that we were no longer in Mummy and Daddy's bed together.

We chose a day, Friday, but the night before he made the move, the last night we ever slept in the same bed, I said to him, "This is the last night we will ever sleep in the same bed." I was trembling and broken.

He went to his side and climbed on top of the covers.

He took me in his arms, killing me—it was the first time I had felt his body in two weeks. I remember listening to his heart beat. I always loved how strong it sounded. And I cried. We cried hard in each other's arms for twenty minutes. I had hopes that the closeness and shared sadness would change him. But it didn't. After our tears ran out, we broke apart and fell asleep. In the morning, I spoke to him again.

"Are we better? Did something change?" I asked. He looked at the ceiling for an eternity.

"No," he said. I continued to wait through another long pause. The tears that were always ready and waiting to come out brimmed up.

"We were saying good-bye and it was heartbreaking. But for me, it doesn't change the certainty I have that I can't be in this marriage anymore," he said.

Then I got pissed.

"Well, I wasn't saying good-bye! For Christ's sake, Josiah, I don't want this marriage to end. I don't want it to end. And I can't fucking believe you do."

"Isabel, I won't talk to you if you are going to take that stance and become out of control." He got out of bed. "I won't talk about this like this. It's destructive and unnecessary," he said, and was almost out of the room.

"Wait! Wait . . . goddamn it. What the fuck do you think this is? You can't just walk out on our family, on the boys, on me. You just can't fucking do it. It's barbaric and wrong and most importantly you swore to me and God and everyone we know that you never fucking would! You have a promise to keep. You have to get through whatever is happening to you—and I think it's fucking

Sylvia—and you have to stay the course. That is what marriage is," I said.

"I can't, Isabel. That is all I can say right now. And I would leave Sylvia out of this. This is between you and me." He stood at the bedroom door and I sat on the edge of the bed for what felt like a long time.

"Josiah," I said.

"What?"

"If you want a separation you have to ask me for one formally," I said. My father had told me that was true.

"What do you mean?"

"I don't want this marriage to end. So if you want to end it, you have to ask me to. It has to be official," I said, head down.

"I understand." We knew we were talking about lawyerly stuff, but neither one of us had actually ever brought up anything legal.

"I want a separation," he said.

I started to cry and went into the bathroom. He went in to check on James, who had been making noises in his crib. We all eventually started up the day as if nothing had happened.

32

Josiah was out of the house a lot. We continued to go through our usual routine in the morning, getting the boys ready for the day and driving Wallace to day care. I would drive Josiah to the office with James at nine, and then I wouldn't see him again until six. He would come home, help get the boys to bed, and then leave again for the office, not returning until around one or two in the morning. I got so little time with him. I remember slowing down the car unnecessarily so that we would miss the green light and we could sit together for the forty-five seconds of red. I felt desperate for more time and wasn't getting any. Josiah structured everything in his life so he was around me as little as possible. I tried to steal time, surprise him. I would drop by his office unexpectedly to discuss a phone bill or ask him to help me with a teaching question. He looked pained to be around me and bored, like a teenager wanting to go out at night but being made to stay home for family dinner. He wasn't there even when he was there. If the conversation led to where we were in our marriage it would ignite quickly into a fight and he would clam up instantly and then leave. He left a lot, and of course I was consumed by wanting to know where he was all day and night when he wasn't actually in a classroom.

My job of being a detective, although time consuming and painful, was not very hard. There was evidence all over the place that Josiah was not in love with me, and more that he was in love with somebody else.

Josiah was being obsessive and very meticulous about how he dressed and looked. Even though we were sleeping in different rooms there were only so many mirrors in the house and I could see him primping. He would carefully look at his hairline and check out his clothes, but the weirdest thing that he did was smile in the mirror. When I saw him do this (which he never did before) I instantly recognized it as something people do when they have a crush. I used to do it myself. You give yourself a smile in the mirror, maybe fantasizing that you are having a casual conversation with the object of your desire. But you are definitely checking to see how *they* are seeing you.

"What are you doing?" I said to him as accusingly as I could. He was mortified at getting busted.

"Nothing. Jesus, Isabel. I was remembering something funny that Ward said." He was appalled that I had seen him.

"You looked weird and I know what you were doing," I said. I was on the sofa watching *Sesame Street* with the boys.

"I wasn't doing anything. Jesus, Isabel. I hate you." He didn't actually say "I hate you," but he did with his eyes. It's like I turned into his mother. I actually am not sure that his mother would ever have busted him on something like that. She is very supportive of her children and more formal. She doesn't make a lot of personal comments. I felt like a mother, but not his.

One time I had called Josiah at the office to talk about something that I made up. During the conversation I heard his office door close. In a second I knew it was Sylvia.

"What was that?" I said.

"What?"

"I heard the door close, someone must have been in there and closed it," I said. He paused.

"It was Sylvia. She wanted a tea bag."

"I didn't hear her speak."

"No, she just looked in, gestured for a tea bag when she saw I was on the phone, got one, and left."

"I think that's weird."

"Isabel . . ." he said.

"No, let me tell you why. If I was Sylvia and wanted a tea bag, first of all I would knock and she didn't because I would have heard it. Then I would say out loud or in a whisper, 'Oh, sorry—is it okay if I grab a tea bag?' And you would say out loud, 'Oh, hi, Sylvia—I'm just talking to Isabel.' At which point you would say in the phone to me, 'Sylvia just walked in, hold on while I get her a tea bag.' She would hear you say that and would say, 'Oh, don't worry, don't get up, I'll just grab one, thanks!' And before she closed the door she would say, 'Say hi to Isabel.' Because she is my friend," I said.

"That accusation is so crazy and off that I won't even respond."

"Really."

"Yes, I have to go teach now."

"You know what I think happened?"

"What?"

"I think she opened the door to your office and before she could say anything, you signaled that it was me on the phone and she got it and closed the door quietly, hoping that I wouldn't hear it," I said. "And I know I'm right."

"I have to go," he said.

"Fine," I said. And slammed down the phone.

33

Of course I thought I was right, but I couldn't get real evidence to know 100 percent. It made me crazy and obsessed. I just kept thinking that if I knew for sure, I could stop it. I could move our family away to Italy for a semester and rip Sylvia and Josiah apart, stop the runaway train. Anytime I called the office and the phone went straight to voice mail I was sure he was talking to her. I would walk by the English department over and over again, hoping I might see them through the window. I noticed everything that Sylvia wore. One time I saw her in salmon-colored high heels and a fifties type skirt. It's true people dressed up to teach, including me, but she looked like she was going to a cocktail party in a Bette Davis movie. I saw her because I was in Secca's office. I often visited Secca on the way back from teaching my class. Although she was young and didn't have children yet, she had a motherly vibe. Her office felt like a home. She had added soft colors to it with throws and pillows. She could offer you a cup of herbal tea in a delicate china cup. Her office was feminine, like herself. Secca was very polite and always welcomed me in. She knew I was having a hard time, although I felt that she was playing two sides of the field. I would make up reasons to go and talk to her, which I enjoyed, but if I'm honest, I was spying. I wanted to know what everyone else in the English department thought of me and Josiah and Sylvia. One Wednesday afternoon in mid-October, I was in Secca's office. Sylvia didn't know I was in there, or I'm sure she wouldn't have come in. But she did. In her salmon shoes.

"Oh, hi," she said.

"Hi," both Secca and I said.

"Wow, look at you! You look nice. Who are you dressing for?" I said, looking her straight in the eye.

"What? Nobody," she said.

"Uh-huh," I said, still looking at her. Secca instantly distracted herself with a zipper. She hated getting dragged into all of this, but there was nothing to be done about it. She was in our tiny community and this affected everyone in it.

"You know, there's a new movie at the movie theater. You guys want to go tonight?" I said.

"I can't," said Secca, "Ward's sister is coming tonight."

"Neither can I, I'm afraid. I've got to work on my job market stuff," said Sylvia.

"Oh, please, Sylvia, it's an hour and a half. We'll eat popcorn and you can count it as dinner. You have to have dinner," I said.

"Well, okay," she said. I had trapped her. And she knew it.

"Good," I said. "Josiah can take care of the boys. He hasn't been around much lately."

There was a really awkward feeling in the room, but I chose to ignore it and gathered my things.

"Meet you in the seats," I said. The early show always started at seven so there was no need to clarify the time.

The movie was *In Her Shoes* with Cameron Diaz. I got there first and bought popcorn. Then Sylvia showed up.

I was having a hard time figuring out what I was doing in that theater with Sylvia. I had two beliefs. One was that Sylvia and Josiah were in love, probably not sleeping together, but in love. And the other was what I had been told by them, which was that they were just friends, and the reason why Josiah was leaving me was because he just couldn't be in our marriage anymore. Sitting next to her was so weird. Was she my friend helping me out in a time of need? Or was she the "Other Woman" who was falling deeply in love with my husband? I swear to God I had no idea.

Things were stilted. Maybe we chatted about a new brand of thong that was all the rage. Maybe we talked about her job search. When the previews started and we were quiet, my mind shot back to my marriage, of course.

"The thing is," I whispered to her during the second preview. "The thing is, I can understand how a man can leave a woman. One adult leaving another, but how can anyone leave Wallace and James?"

When I said this I had an image of James standing in the kitchen with a big pear that he had been hauling around.

And then in her half-French accent Sylvia said the most dumbfounding thing. "It happens every day."

What?????? Fifteen thousand bells went off in my head. The words just hung in the air. *Happens every day.*

No woman says that. Of all the female friends I had told about Josiah's decision to leave me, not one woman had said anything remotely like that. At the burrito shop, when I told Rebecca that he was leaving, she burst into tears and instantly took my hand across the table and didn't let go for three entire minutes. When I told Janet, the house cleaner, earlier that week, she stopped in the middle of folding Wallace's PJs, looked me in the eyes, and grabbed me in her arms and gave me a life-ending hug until I was really uncomfortable. Many, many, many friends said that he wouldn't actually do it. Some people got off-the-charts mad, lots cried, like our babysitter Grace. *Nobody* but Sylvia said *it happens every day.*

Then I knew. I was told I was wrong by both Josiah and Sylvia for the next couple of months, but that was the moment I knew in my heart of hearts that Josiah was not alone in his mission to leave the marriage. He had a partner urging him on, and that partner was Sylvia.

34

October break was coming up the last week in the month, and we had decided that we would take the time to go to New York, stay with my parents, and do five days of heavy-duty emergency couples therapy with our old therapist, Dr. Bergen. It had been about three weeks since the rocking-chair moment. Josiah has a strong interest in and respect for psychotherapy, and even if he single-mindedly wanted out of the marriage, he would never end a marriage without talking to somebody first, even if it was a formality.

We had bought tickets to fly to New York, but when the day actually came we got a phone call from Josiah's mother. There was a big storm brewing down South that was supposed to hit New York later on that evening. Julia is so obsessed with air travel and weather I think they should give her an on-camera job at the Weather Channel and it would cut down on overcrowded flights forever because she would convince everyone not to fly. Even though we knew this about her and knew the drive was twelve hours, and even though the airports had nothing to report about canceled flights, we took her advice and decided to drive. People say that when you are in the midst of a tragedy or under huge stress you should not make any decisions because they will probably be ill-fated. The decision to drive was a humdinger. Two boys under four, a dog, and two miserably sad, quasi-unmarried parents in a minivan together for twelve hours and a storm lurking somewhere along the East Coast. When we set out we only knew of one storm. We were unaware of a rogue October blizzard coming across the midsection of the country and zooming toward us from behind as well.

Josiah and I were barely speaking to each other as we loaded the boys and the dog into the minivan and took off out of town with the worst plan of the year and no provisions to implement it. As we passed the airport in Cleveland (the flight to New York from Cleveland takes one hour and every plane left that day) the video player that was built into the car went dead. Lots of people, parents of young children especially, when they read this might call out aloud, "Go to the nearest Wal-Mart and buy a $120 DVD player!!!" Like it was a horror movie and you see the unknowing woman make the wrong turn into the part of the house where the killer is. But because we were deep in the swamp of poor decision making we chose to think that the radio would be sufficient entertainment for the boys and we drove on.

The only subject on both our minds was our marriage, but because our darling boys were two feet away from us and we didn't want them to hear any talk of an impending divorce, we just stayed quiet. Actually, just Josiah kept quiet while I sang songs, made animal noises, and doled out almonds and graham crackers conservatively because we didn't think to pack a lot of food on this crazy ride. Hours went by, the boys took naps, and as we entered the mountains of Pennsylvania, the skies darkened.

I guess it was because we were in the mountains or maybe it was just because of the way our luck was going that month, but within about forty-five minutes of being in the mountains a walloping blizzard hit those parts with a force that I had never seen before. The wind howled around us, the snow was flying by the windows horizontally. All the trees were breaking either because of the power of the wind or because of the weight of the snow that had instantly piled up on every branch. Wallace and James were quiet as mice, with the exception of one remark from Wallace.

"Mama, look at all those broken trees," he said.

I did look at all the broken trees. I was frightened in every way I could be, and all those broken trees looked to me like my life. Our tree was bent over and broken. I didn't think I would be able to fix it even though I desperately wanted to.

And then the already slow-moving traffic came to a stop. A tree had blown over across the highway and nobody could go anywhere. At first we could move a little bit forward, and when we did we heard a weird scratchy, bumpy noise from under the car.

"What is that?" Josiah said.

"I don't know, but I am so freaked out," I said quietly.

"That is not a good noise. Can you hear it?" he said.

I listened.

"It sounds like we are running over something," I said.

Josiah got out of the car. When he opened the door a small gale came in and made the boys shriek. When the door closed everything was silent again. The dog jumped into my lap.

"Fuck, goddamn it!" Josiah said as he hurled himself into the car again. "The fucking tire is flat. It's shredded."

"Oh my God," I said.

"What happened?" Wallace said.

"Nothing, sugar, the tire just busted," I said to him in a fake calm voice.

"We have a spare, I think," Josiah said.

"Where?" I said.

It is amazing that I even knew what a spare was. At that moment I could not have been less proud of my lack of knowledge about cars.

"I think it's under the car somewhere in the middle," he said.

"What the fuck, do you not know where it is?" I said, losing my cool.

"Calm down, Isabel, I do. I'll find it . . . Goddamn it!" he said, and pounded the steering wheel.

I looked at our one cell phone and of course it had only one bar of power and reception.

It was all unreal. I honestly think that if a murderer had run up the side of the road out of the storm and killed all of us in our car I would not be surprised. I started to lose my breath. We had no water and about seventeen almonds left to get us through the night should we have to stay that long. The dog knew more than the boys that we were in a bit of a pickle and started getting fidgety. She was jumping from the back to the front and then back again, thankfully amusing the children but driving me insane.

Josiah zipped up his jacket and went outside. He had to get the spare tire out from under the floorboard of the car where the children's feet were dangling. He pulled the side door open and started to dig through the tote bags of diapers and garbage bags of McDonald's and maneuvered the floor around.

"There it is," he said. I know had I been by myself I would absolutely not have found that tire.

Josiah proceeded to change the tire. I watched him out of my side mirror. I looked at him, with the snow building up on his black hair and with no gloves, and thought *I love you.* I loved that he knew how to change a tire. I loved how he could read directions in even the hardest manuals and complete them correctly. I loved that even though we were in the middle of a raging storm far away from everything safe that we knew, I trusted that he would change that tire. He was able. I also knew that he was getting us to New York not to save our marriage but to end it under the guidance of a professional. He could fix the tire in the middle of a blizzard, but he wouldn't even try to fix our marriage. I couldn't make him love me again even though I was the mother of his two little blond boys, being very good in the backseat.

Two and a half hours later the traffic started to move and we creeped our way to a small village called Danville that by the grace of God had an auto parts shop that we caught two minutes before they were to close at five. The spare tire we had was the small doughnut kind. The workers in the shop were disappointed to see us come in for a new tire. They were obviously leaving to go to a wedding or big party. Some of them were in tuxes. There was a motel in the town as well, where we spent the night. The kids had never slept in a hotel before and were beside themselves with joy. Josiah slept in one queen bed with James and I slept in the other with Wallace. By the morning the skies were clear and we headed back on the road, making it to New York by lunchtime.

35

This is a good time to bring up other people's perception of us and what was going on. As awful as it was living with the eruption of our marriage, I was adapting to it as a way of life. But after a while I realized that other people might have had their own perceptions. If I suddenly burst into tears in the copy shop, it didn't throw me, but it sure threw the copy shop guy. Josiah, Wallace, James, and I were living in an alternate universe, very different from the one we were living in a month before. I guess it would be like if your house got flooded. You would be shocked and undone by how wet everything was, but after a short while you would get on with the process of cleaning everything up instead of sitting around amazed by how wet everything was. *However,* if your mother came over and saw for the first time how drenched your life was she might have a big, new reaction about the state of affairs. You would be ahead of her—you would be in a more advanced place or at least further along. That's what I felt like a lot of the time. Ahead of my friends and family.

Coming home to my parents' apartment with Josiah and our boys, knowing that my marriage was over, felt like coming home from boarding school after being expelled for drinking in the woods. Shame. I felt ashamed, and like a pain in the neck. Nobody would say that I had anything to be ashamed of. Josiah was leaving me and although I was trying with all my might to stop him, it wasn't working. I felt ashamed and I'm sure Josiah did too. We were a mess, and it was going to take a lot of help to clean it up. With the purchase of our new house and both of us in gainful employment at Oberlin College, we had just earned independence that had taken a long time to achieve. Our parents had probably just a month before crossed us off the worry list and were moving on to some other child. And then out of nowhere we were there again, but this time at the very very top of that list.

My mother can't hide anything, and the second we walked in the door, I could see the strain and hyperconcern on her face. The looks on my parents' faces made me feel like we were the cast of *Les Misérables* walking into the apartment. My children were dressed in pathetic street-urchin rags. I was Cosette, the innocent victim. And Josiah was Javert, public enemy number one. I don't think they even looked at Josiah. We were there to go to the doctor, though, so everyone was holding out hope that Dr. Bergen would work her magic and they would be able to pack us back into the Odyssey at the end of our five days, fixed. I hoped for that too and was getting more and more afraid by the day that it just was not going to happen.

The reality of New York frightened me. I knew that if

we couldn't bust through this "rough patch," as everyone was calling it, I would have to live there again.

Oh my goodness, New York. It felt so big. As easy and enjoyable as it is walking down the little empty paths of Oberlin, the New York streets—even though I had grown up on them—felt impossibly impossible. I had two little country mice in my nest, and the loud, busy streets of the Upper West Side, my Upper West Side, were terrifying to them. You had to cross a big street to see grass, nobody said hello to you on the sidewalk, it was cold and hard and scary. They must have been so uneasy. Their parents were distracted to the point of being absent, they had gotten stuck in a terrible blizzard on a mountain in a scary car. Their grandparents talked in hushed tones most of the time and then would compensate by being overly enthusiastic. Wallace and James must have thought their world was coming to an end. They were right.

It was unbearable. It was unbearable to think about then and it's unbearable to think about now, to think about just how awful it is for your children when a marriage ends. I don't know about when a marriage ends and the kids are older. Some of my friends say that they were relieved when their parents finally divorced and lived separately. I'm not talking about that. I had young children and the very last thing that they wanted was for their parents to live apart. It breaks their hearts. Heartbreak at age three is too hard. It feels unnatural. You tell yourself they will get used to it, and they do to a certain extent, but they always feel something sad about it. I felt so sad that I was unable to stop the truck that was about to hit them. I told myself that because I would make sure they survived it, they would gain incredible coping skills for the future. They would learn from an early age that nothing in life is easy. That there is pain and heartache. That you have to miss people much more than you ever want to and tolerate less than perfect circumstances much more than you ever think you have to. But they would get strong from it, and strength is good.

But it is so sad. It makes you so very sad. I didn't want them to hate their father. I wanted them to be proud of their father. He was half of who they were, and I was not going to risk them feeling bad about themselves because their mother was angry at their father. It wasn't their fault that Josiah had fallen out of love with me, and just because that was true, I didn't feel it gave me the right to be bitter and hateful, especially if it could save my kids from feeling bitter and hateful. I rejected anger. I felt that it was okay to be sad. They could handle sad. I could handle sad. Sad was organic and could change and decompose, but anger was like plastic and would sit, refusing to change or go away. Anger wasn't going to serve anyone. Josiah refused to speak to me if I was angry and I couldn't bear not speaking to the man I loved no matter how much he was hurting me. I felt embarrassed to be angry, like it was dirty. I couldn't think when I was angry. It was hard and there was a lot to be mad about—really mad—but I found that anger is hard to live with. I can't even boil an egg when I am angry. I couldn't breathe and I certainly couldn't mother. I had to find times and places to be angry so it didn't come out in some weird way later, but it had to be thought about and acted out carefully and privately so my children didn't feel it. I think some people might have thought I was taking it lying down, but that wasn't the case. I just didn't want to rant and be a crazy divorcée. I wanted to keep my family a family, just in a different shape. Josiah was the father of my boys and I wanted them to feel like that was a very good thing. I wanted to keep our happy years alive for them. If I couldn't forgive my husband, I could forgive the father of my children.

People did not understand this. Dear friends of mine, who were trying so hard to help me and who were so upset by the turn of events, thought I was in some major denial.

"Oh, you'll get angry soon enough, and you should be fucking angry," a pal of mine said on the phone.

I just didn't want to, and why should I? Couldn't I handle the end of my marriage the way I wanted to? Did my friends want me to suffer more than I already was suffering? The answer to that, from friends to family, was no. And some of the time, I was rip-roaring mad.

36

Our shrink couldn't reach Josiah. For him to say he was willing to keep trying would have been progress. We went for five days and nothing changed. He just kept saying, "I can't." Or, "I won't." I really did not understand the "I just can't do it." In my mind our marriage, our entire life, for that matter, wasn't something I had a choice about. It just was. Like having blue eyes or thick hair. Maybe he always felt that he was choosing to be in it or choosing to "do it" and then one day (the day that Sylvia walked in the teachers' room) he decided that he couldn't choose to do it any longer. I really couldn't believe that it was so bad, and neither could Dr. Bergen.

At some point in a session Josiah said to Dr. Bergen, with tears streaming down his face, "Isabel should be married to someone like Clark Jackson."

"Who is Clark Jackson?" she said.

"He's our friend, well, my old old friend," I said, a little taken aback.

"He is a really nice guy. He is straightforward and kind and good. He's just a good guy," Josiah said.

"He's not that complicated," I said.

"Yeah," said Josiah.

"Do you think I'm not deep enough for you?"

"No, no . . . that's not it, it's just that you and Clark are more alike than we are."

"Clark would never leave his wife and children," I said.

"If you and Clark were together you might not have the kinds of complications we have," he said.

I wanted to say, "You mean *Sylvia*?" But knowing that saying it would start a fight and seeing as he was opening up, I didn't. And for that reason, I don't think we covered Sylvia in those sessions. We focused on just the two of us.

"I still don't get what kinds of complications are so bad you are willing to destroy everything we have built to get away from them," I said.

"We are just so different. And you and Clark are more alike," he said.

"Let's try to remember that even though you might feel that Clark would be a better husband for Isabel, *you* and Isabel are in fact married," Dr. Bergen said.

"Yeah!" I said. "What the fuck, Josiah? And Clark is married to Wendy, so this is a stupid conversation."

But what our sessions got to was the fact that Josiah honestly felt that he and I were different. And I could see his point sometimes. The most obvious, but maybe overly simplistic, difference between us was that Josiah was dark and I was light. He was the seal swimming in the shadows and the shoals, and I was the orangutan swinging through the branches. But nobody can be only dark or only light. It's shortsighted to think like that and dangerous because you get pigeonholed. I made the argument that I too can feel despaired, hopeless, and frightened. "I'm dark . . . I am!" But there were other differences too. He felt he was too much like his father—aloof, selfish, irresponsible—and I was too much like my mother—practical, empirical, and judgmental. It's not that either of us had problems with our parents, it's the way we were like them that caused us trouble. He was right, I can be judgmental. Sometimes I did boss him around unfairly, especially where the children were concerned. "Get me that milk, will you? Hurry!" And I do have a tendency to think the way I did things was the right way. But like my mother, I am good at looking at my less than perfect behavior and trying my hardest to improve it. When I say I am sorry it comes along with all my good intentions to work on myself. In those sessions, I was digging deep to find out how I could change and get him back, in case all of this wasn't about Sylvia.

And there was plenty to work on. Although I try hard not to be, I am also a micromanager. It can come out subtly, like how one should slice a carrot, or how soon a thank-you note should be written, but it can be more invasive than that too. The worst micromanaging I ever did to Josiah was tell him how to dedicate his book. Josiah wrote an academic book that was published. It's hard to publish an academic book, so it was really exciting when it happened. One day, as the publication time approached, I asked him about it, without thinking the question through first.

"You get to have a dedication?" I said.

"Yeah, it's a book, you know," he said cheerfully.

"Oh. Well, who are you dedicating it to?"

"I was thinking, to the boys."

"The boys?" I said a little too forcefully.

"Yes," he said.

"Oh," I said with hurt feelings.

"I am going to say something about you in the dedication too."

"No, that's not what I meant," I said, totally embarrassed that he had picked up what I had been feeling. "It's just that they weren't even born for most of the time that you were writing it."

"Ian was," he said.

"I know, but he was a baby. He's just a kid, it's not like he helped you, lived through it with you, believed in you even in the hard moments." I couldn't stop myself.

"I guess you are right."

"I mean, I'm not telling you who you should dedicate your own book to." Yes I was.

"No, no, I'll rethink it," he said.

He ended up writing me a beautiful dedication. I loved it, but every time I have read it since, I can't help thinking that I forced him to do it.

So I can be a micromanager, like my mother, but he can be a rule breaker, like his father, Sherman. Not that he doesn't abide by the law. He's a social rule breaker. Josiah's father is handsome, like Josiah, and comes from a very old and distinguished southern family. He has an upper-class, melodic southern accent, is an avid reader, and wears a gold family ring on his pinky. He and his wife, Susan, have been good friends with my parents ever since they bought a house in Maine in the early 1970s to be closer to Josiah and his brother, whose mother and stepfather had bought a house in Maine the year before. So, to be clear, Josiah's parents were divorced and remarried by the time Josiah was four. By the time he was six, both couples had bought houses on the same tiny island off the coast of Maine so both sets of parents could be closer to the children during the summer. It was the same island that my mother's family has had a house on for one hundred years.

So anyway, I have known Josiah's parents and stepparents since I was a young girl. As I grew up and became aware that families had different personalities, I thought that Josiah's family had a personality I really liked. They were fun, full of life. They weren't uptight like some other families in Maine. At club picnics their food always looked good and there was a lot of it. Susan, Josiah's stepmother, is a marvelous entertainer. She can sew beautiful children's clothes and make old-fashioned southern food like chess pie. She has a knack for setting tables in divine ways nobody else would think of. She was also a southern beauty queen. (A lot of good-looking people in that bunch.) They have a lot of style and charm. From the outside they seemed like the coolest family on the block. They used to have these "story nights" where the family and some friends would gather around a huge campfire that the men would spend the day preparing. Everyone who came was asked to bring a story. You could make the story up, you could read a chapter of a book, or it could be famous lore from your family. There were hot dogs and deviled eggs, kids, and lots of wine. Sherman held court and Susan wore a summer hat, wild with flowers and ribbons, that she pulled out of her closet every year for the occasion. The stories were applauded, especially when a courageous child took a turn. The evenings went well into the night and felt like the very best of what a family could be. And then I got to be a part of all of it. I even got to have their last name.

Josiah's father knows everything about birds and sailing. He is a lawyer, but he could have been a professor, as he becomes deeply involved with the subjects that interest him, making himself an expert—almost obsessed. Although he can be massively charming and endearing, and almost always was supremely kind to me, he also can be very difficult. He tends to play by his own rules and although I know he doesn't mean to, if he doesn't like the conventional way things are going, he'll just do his own thing, not thinking through how it may hurt someone. I could think of a few examples of this, but I guess the most illuminating one was that he had left his wife, Josiah's mother, for Susan, Josiah's stepmother, while she was pregnant with Josiah. Of course, it was long ago and complicated and I don't know all the facts, but the story was there and it haunted me. It all worked out. As a family I really believe they've worked it out. There is lots of love, and lots of effort. But it always scared me that Josiah was like his father in that one very significant way.

But with those true things about us, and differences between us, in all the sessions the doctor gave us many examples of how similar we actually were, the first and most important being that we both loved and adored our shared children. We were both teachers, we loved Oberlin, we loved our dog. She was trying to save our marriage. It was in vain.

The last night in New York Josiah and I went to the movies with my best friend, Bess, and her husband, George. Again, the feeling of doing a normal couple thing with a normal couple when you are in the stratosphere of abnormal is really uncomfortable. The movie ended with one of the lead characters getting MS or some other kind of horrific degenerative disease. The character's lovely husband was by her side the entire time the poor woman was dying. I sat there and just could not believe that if I got some horrible, painful disease when I was a little older, I wasn't going to have my faithful, stalwart husband there to feed me water and pat my leg! He was sitting right next to me now, but it was temporary. He wasn't going to be there if a terrible illness befell me. What about in sickness and in health? Wasn't it a guarantee that if you got married you got the leg pats in the life-ending moments? No, it wasn't. My heart sank to yet another rung that I didn't think existed. And then I felt Bess take my hand.

Just before Josiah and I got in the cab, Bess hugged me hard and whispered, "It's not going to happen. It's going to be all right."

I looked at her and subtly shook my head. The next day we drove back to Ohio. The drive is a blur to me. I was soaking in the fact that therapy hadn't worked and what that meant for me and the boys. There were no snowstorms or flat tires to make the trip stand out. There was this wolf, though. As we were entering Ohio, I swear I saw a wolf on the side of the road. It probably was a coyote, but at the time it looked like a huge silver wolf howling on the side of the road.

Part Three

Wallace and James

37

Josiah's talking so much about how different and ill-suited we were started to get to me. One half of me really didn't care if we were the odd couple—we were married, we had children, and we had to stick to our guns and make it work. Not to mention that if you had asked me four months before all this happened to rate our marriage from 1 to 10, I would have given us an 8. But there was another part of me that started to imagine what it would be like to be with someone who was more like me, and who loved who I was. I didn't let myself go too far in these fantasies because, one, I thought God or somebody might be listening in. It felt adulterous even to imagine what life would be like not married to Josiah. And, two, because it was piercing to think that Josiah actually didn't love me, which was really becoming a convincing notion. That he had just fallen out of love with me. I had one impulse to fight and make him love me again and another to move on. Just jump in and get with another program. You can't make people love you, I told myself. But I did love him, so it felt unnatural and mean to take the move-on steps. I was split down the middle. The first step for moving on is to get a really good lawyer. A productive step to take in trying to save your marriage is to eliminate the woman who is getting between you and your husband. I had to do both.

My father got a big-shot New York lawyer friend of his to recommend lawyers in Cleveland. Dad called me and in hushed tones read me the list of five.

Jack Jones: A killer bulldog who will rip the guy to shreds and leave no prisoners.

Whoa, I thought.

Jane Jones: A shark who will get you anything you want if you leave her alone to do the dirty work.

John Jones: Smart, can play hardball or not, depending on what you want.

James Jones: Big firm, will get the job done.

Sara Jones: Perfectly nice.

Hummmm. I wrote everything down word for word and then read over each description when I was sure that Josiah was out of the house (which was most of the time). I didn't want him to know I was getting a lawyer. I was told by my father and a number of girlfriends that I should keep him in the dark until I was ready to start negotiating. I was given a lot of advice from a lot of people. Get my own bank account, get a private investigator, freeze assets (what assets?), start to hide the jewelry (what jewelry?), get another email account. All of the advice, although I appreciated it, sometimes made me feel like I was in a spy movie, which freaked me out. Even if he was doing all of that, I wasn't going to. We didn't have much. Maybe if we were loaded, living in Scarsdale, with a few houses, multiple bank accounts, and boats coming out of our ears, I would have felt more compelled to take action. But we lived in Ohio and he was a schoolteacher. He was probably having an affair, but did I really want to see some detective's photographs of him, my husband, darting out of her apartment in the late hours of the night? Or worse, of him and Sylvia giggling over tea in her office? No. I could do my own snooping and investigating. If this marriage was really ending, I wanted to end it with dignity. But I wanted to get it right too.

I chose John Jones, smart, can play hardball or not. I thought he would listen to us. I didn't want Josiah to fry. What would Wallace and James think if their father fried? I just didn't want to be that woman. Lawyers can make you crazy, and I had enough going on. I didn't need insanity too.

38

When I was a little girl in Dark Harbor, Maine, my brother Andrew and I used to wake up very early. It was usually foggy, especially in the morning. I would lie in my little room with the rosebud wallpaper and stare out the window at the pine tree that stood on the edge of the small cliff that dropped off to the water's edge. You couldn't see the sea because of the fog, but you could hear it. The sound I remember most is the sound of a Boston Whaler in the distance heading out somewhere.

My brother, who is two years younger than I am, would come in, not say anything, and then the two of us would head into the living room to listen to *Snow White and the Seven Dwarves* on a little red and white record player. On the other side of the record was *Riki Ticki Tavi,* but we always started out with *Snow White.* I guess we were waiting until my mother called us into breakfast, but I don't remember waking my parents. The living room was closer to where our two older brothers were sleeping. They were teenagers (and from my father's first marriage to Joy, whose name really should have been Serenity) and slept all the time. My father believes that because teenagers are growing at such a fast pace, they should be allowed to sleep as much as they want. I feel like none of us ever had to wake up early in the summertime, though we must have at some point, because we all learned how to sail and those classes were in the morning. But in general the rule was never wake a sleeping teenager. No good ever comes of it.

The *Snow White* recording started off with this man saying, "Hi, boys and girls, you want to hear a story about Snow White and the Seven Dwarves? [*long pause*] Gooood." He said "gooood" in a groovy, 1970s way.

Andrew and I would sit on either side of the sofa and listen to *Snow White* and then *Riki Ticki Tavi,* over and over and over. We eventually would be rousted out by my mother, fed, and taken to play tennis on a soggy clay court or learn knots on the yacht club dock. Eventually, later in the day, we would see our brothers Dave and Doug. My brothers for most of the seventies hung out with the Fenton boys. The Fentons were three brothers named Peter, Paul, and Mark, and each one was better looking than the next. All of them, including my brothers, had long hair that fell below their collarbones. Sometimes they had to babysit for me, and those were the best times of my life. I would put on a pretty nightgown and make each one of them read me a chapter of a Laura Ingalls Wilder book. It was how I learned to flirt. (What's better when you are six than a sixteen-year-old boy reading you *Little House in the Big Woods*?)

When my little brother and I would encounter our big

brothers, who were probably at our house with the Fentons making their breakfast at two in the afternoon, they would give us never-ending shit about the record.

"Hey, boys and girls," Dave would mock, "you wanna hear a story about two little kids who got tossed in the ocean? Goooood." And then all the teenagers would laugh and bring their mountains of food to the Adirondack chairs outside to eat and look at the bay.

We pretended to be scared that we had woken them up with our record at 6:45 a.m., but this happened every day of the summer. I don't know about Andrew, but I loved having lots of brothers and their pals in the house. I think my parents liked it too.

When your marriage falls apart, some very distinct things happen to you. One is you lose about twenty pounds very quickly. There is even a line about it in a Paul Simon song. I was eating normally but losing weight as if I were on a nonstop juice fast. Ironically, even though you feel terrible, you start to look pretty. Maybe it's God's way of gearing you up to go back into the dating world.

You start to look to the tiniest things to make you feel better, alive. Anything to give you even a moment of happiness. My friend Eve told me to look at the fallen leaf on the road and try to see even the smallest glimpse of beauty. Notice the good song on the radio. Your kid's smile might do it, but to me the wonderful smiles of Wallace and James were heartbreaking.

But I did try to notice the small stuff. One Sunday morning the four of us were at brunch. It was painful. We were faking being a family. I held the belief that if we still did family things together, perhaps Josiah would come back down to earth and see he was making a godawful decision. He was miserable. The place where we were having brunch was actually the town bar, but on Sundays a renegade brunch cook took over the kitchen that usually slung out frozen bar food. He produced world-class eggs and pancakes. His specialty was savory pancakes. I ordered pancakes with asparagus, Gruyère, and ham. They were served with maple syrup and two eggs on top. It was a leap of culinary faith to order them. Once we got our food and I had started the boys off on their plain pancakes and Josiah's head was fixed firmly down on his omelet, I did what the waiter told me to and poured the syrup over the dish. It was sublime. Something about the sweet and savory and the sharp cheese and the runny yolks. I called out, "Sweet lord, these are incredible!" And I started to laugh. It was as if I was eating dulce de leche ice cream for the first time. A bomb of involuntary happiness went off in my mouth. Josiah didn't seem to appreciate my enthusiasm, and the boys continued to throw hash browns on the floor and dump the salt on the table, but at that very moment my life was being saved.

I thought if I could get such a kick out of these pancakes, I hadn't died. He hadn't killed me or destroyed my ability to take pleasure in life. I could taste something heavenly and feel joy, even if only for a second. That pancake meant I would be okay. It gave me courage and hope that even on the darkest day, there is a way to see light and feel the beauty of the world. Sounds corny, but life can be glorious. Remembering that during the lowest, saddest times is imperative if you want to get back to the highs. But you have to look. You have to remember to remind yourself to look.

Even though the pancake thing was illuminating for a moment, I still had a long way to go.

39

For about six days, Josiah and I tiptoed around each other, overly polite one moment and then cold and distant another. Strangers with children. We tried to do normal things together with Wallace and James, promising not to fight with them around. It was November and getting cold. The empty, stark playgrounds of the parks department of northeast Ohio could not have been a more depressing backdrop for our outings. The two of us would push the children on the swings, breaking silence only to compliment a boy on a high swing or make the "Wheeeeeeeeeeeeeee!" sound when one would come down the slide. Josiah was putting in the dad hours, watching the clock until he could get away from me. I was treasuring every second that all four of us were together, no matter how strained it was. He didn't spend any time at all hanging around if he didn't have to. Once we were home, he would turn around and go to the office. Because both of my parents worked full-time, it's built into my psyche that you really can't question the validity of "the office." Since the office was where he spent virtually all his time, I found any reason I could to go there.

One of the really nice friends with children I had was a Norwegian woman, Liv, who was married to the cello professor at the conservatory. They had a big house down the street from us and three daughters. Like most mothers in Oberlin, she had not a lick of help. She mothered beautifully. Her kitchen was always full of art projects and something vegetarian simmering on the stovetop. Her kids were sweet and polite. They even had quiet hour, when the girls went to their rooms to play—and they actually went happily and didn't come down until the hour was up. I don't think I could pay either one of my boys mountains of ice cream for all eternity to play by themselves for sixty minutes in their rooms.

Liv, like everyone, was astonished at my predicament. She hosted playdates with the kids, and was a sounding board for me. She left tins of delicious Norwegian treats in my kitchen whenever her mother sent them from Norway. One day I came home before teaching to find a tin of *pepparkakor,* a traditional Norwegian Christmas treat. They are very thin ginger cookies. Norwegian people believe that if you press your finger in the middle of the wafer and it cracks in half, you will have good luck. I ate twelve, cracking every one first with my pointer finger. If one cracked into six pieces, I would eat all the shards and try again. I cracked about half of them perfectly in two. Fifty-fifty good luck wasn't bad, I thought.

I had to teach but I knew these thin little cookies would be very good with tea. Ahhh, an excuse to go to Josiah's office. Even in the worst of times, we would be able to connect over a good tea biscuit. I carefully wrapped a stack, not wanting to break any before I delivered them, and set out. I made sure to brush my hair and put lipstick on before I went. I wanted so badly for him to think I was pretty. What's better than a pretty woman bringing you cookies *and* she happens to be the mother of your children.

His door was closed and locked. I knew he also had to teach in about twenty minutes, so I waited there thinking he was having a pee or something. When I saw him walking down the hall, I beamed at him and held out the cookies.

"I have something for you," I said.

Like one of those thin, trotting African dogs, he slid away from me and walked close to the wall. There was a water fountain with a garbage pail underneath it. I saw him chuck something into the can. He was trying to be subtle, but really how subtle can you be in a hallway? He pushed past me and opened his door. The smell of smoke was overwhelming.

"Were you smoking?" I almost shouted. He closed the door. "Was that a cigarette butt you threw away?"

He didn't say anything. He didn't look scared, he looked fed up.

"Yes, I was smoking. I started again because of all the stress we are under," he said.

"*You* started smoking?" I said.

Josiah is an obsessive runner. Josiah smoked for six months in college and gave it up. Josiah is not a smoker. There are people in the world who really are smokers, who even look good with a cigarette. Josiah isn't one of those people. I quit smoking when I was twenty-five, but I was a smoker and I know one when I see one and Josiah isn't one.

"I can't believe you. If anyone in this scenario gets to start smoking again, it's me! Not that I ever would because it's vile and lethal and may I remind you we have children to take care of . . . What the fuck are you doing?" My grip was tightening on the cookies.

"I have to teach. I really don't see why this is any of your business," he said.

That was a killer. In two months I had gone from being a wife with full access and open communication with my husband to some kind of stranger with absolutely no rights or access to the man I had been living with for the last six years.

"How is it none of my business, Josiah? We live together," I said, starting to despair.

"Not for long," he said quietly.

40

I pushed the cookies into his hands and ran out of the building. I felt like I had been hit again by that fucking train that hit me a month before. My breathing was short and I couldn't focus my eyes.

What is happening, what is happening?

I made my way into the bathroom of the theater building and splashed water on my face. I have to teach. Focus on teaching. Don't lose it. I walked out into the foyer where the theater students were lying around in their ripped jeans and flannels. Even though I was losing it, I still felt the rush of having students. You are a form of movie star to them even though they would never admit it. They want to talk to you, tease you, brag to you about something they did.

Then I saw the chair of the department, the man who had hired me. Like any good actor, he immediately vibed that something was wrong with me.

"Hi, Isabel. You okay?" he said.

Help is help and I took it. I had not told anyone in my

department what was happening in my life. I didn't want them to know. I didn't want it to get in the way of my work or theirs. But he nailed me and I just headed into his office, sat down on the lumpy, brownish yellow, nubby couch and sobbed. Nothing like a drama teacher to create a safe place for you to let your guard down.

"I just saw Josiah . . . I busted him . . . He had been smoking!" I wailed.

"You don't know this, but he told me six weeks ago he wants to leave us . . . and now he is smoking!" I cried. And then I flopped over on the couch and sobbed until it was out of me. When I sat up and breathed for a while, he said, "When people start smoking, it's usually because they are smoking with someone." I sat straight up.

"Oh my God," I said.

Jim looked at me, reached out, and put his hand on my knee.

"I'm sorry," he said.

Of course that French witch had gotten my husband to start smoking! Now I was on a rampage. It all had seemed like a dream before. Nobody waltzes into town, hands out her syllabus, and proceeds to steal the best-looking, most-married, father-of-two English professor in town—in one month! That can't be real, that can't be my life. But apparently it was. Enough with being surprised by little bits and pieces of gut instinct. Now I needed proof that this was true.

My friend Bess had told me that she would come out from New York on a moment's notice if I needed her. I called that night and by the weekend she was there.

41

Josiah moved into his office at the English department for the weekend so Bess and Oliver, her eight-month-old baby, could have the guest bedroom.

When they arrived, I showed her around our house as if everything was okay. I had been dying for her to see every inch of trim and 1877 detail since we bought the house. We suspended my inconvenient marital problems until we had completed a top-to-bottom tour. We finished in the living room, where the boys were watching a movie and where there was a fantastic armchair that I had covered in a Lulu DK stripe that I was so proud of. Bess put Oliver on the floor with a pile of toys and rummaged in her bag. She pulled out a small brown velvet box and gave it to me. Inside was a perfectly round gold locket on a long chain. I could hardly open it for fear of bursting into tears while the children were in the room. Tears were streaming down Bess's face already. I opened the locket and there were the faces of Wallace and James. I clutched the locket to my chest and buried myself in Bess's arms. It's so hard to cry silently, but we both did, shaking and weeping, surrounded by our kids.

Josiah came home only for a moment to put the boys to bed and then slid out to leave Bess and me to our bottle of wine and scrambled eggs.

"You know what my mother says? She says—no way. No way. You just tell him that it's unacceptable. That he just can't go. It's not right. Only the lowest of the low leaves his children," she said.

"I know, but he says he can't do it anymore and, Bess, I don't know what I can do but believe him and let him go. I just can't stop him," I said. I started to cry.

"It can't be Sylvia," she said.

"I know—right?" I said, and instantly stopped weeping. "He wouldn't leave us just for another woman, right?"

She shook her head. "You never know, though. It might not be that he is in bed with her every night. It could just be a look in the hallway, or the slightest linger of their hands if they exchange a book," she said.

"It could be that maddeningly sexy thing of falling in love with someone you can't have. It's worse than just sex," I said.

"Let's try, try, try to see his side of this and maybe we can get somewhere," she said, with the look on her face of someone who has just been hired to solve a mystery.

"Okay," I said. She drank her wine and thought.

"You remember Lupe?"

"Yes." Lupe was her boyfriend when she lived in Europe during college.

"Lupe really loved me. But he loved this perfect, idealized view of me that frankly, I think he made up most of the time. I was sort of that, but I was also all this other dark stuff that he really wasn't interested in, so he just didn't deal with it. He just raised me up higher and higher and finally *I* couldn't deal with it anymore. It was too good and I knew I wasn't as good as what he wanted me to be. It made me feel strangled and trapped and terrible. So I behaved badly so he could see that I really wasn't so great. I needed someone to see that I was an asshole sometimes and love me anyway," she said.

"But I love Josiah and I know he's an asshole," I said.

"But does he know that? And Isabel, do you really let him be an asshole and accept it without judgment?" she said, raising her eyebrow.

"No. No, I rip him apart and tell him he's worse than his father," I said, panicking.

"Aha. Look, Izzle, marriage is hard and it has many changes and twists. Maybe this is it. Maybe he feels he just can't be himself? Maybe if you really talk to him and open this up, he'll rethink?"

"Do you think I should go now? To the office?" I said, getting up.

"Yes. No. Yes. I'll stay here, you go." We both were excited now, as if we really had the answer.

I drove our minivan out into the cold night to the English department.

I parked in front of his window in the empty parking lot. His light was the only one on. I called his office on my cell phone. There was no answer. What? No answer. I called him on his cell phone, no answer. I ran to the door of the building, but it was locked after ten. I ran back to the car and called the office again. This time he picked up.

"Hi," I said. "It's me."

"Is everything okay?" he said.

"Yeah, I'm outside your office."

"Isabel, I'm going to sleep now."

"Please. Please, Josiah, it's important. Bess and I were talking and I think we came to something important that might help us."

"Okay, I'll be right down." He hung up.

He let me in. He was still in his clothes. We went through the dim hallway, so weird to be in there at night, like if someone let you into the A&P after dark.

He let me into his office. On the floor was a pillow and a duvet folded in half like a sleeping bag. I started to cry.

"I hate that you are sleeping in here. I hate this so much . . . Just listen to me, okay?" I said.

"Yes, but, Isabel, it's late—Bess is with all three boys?" This made me mad.

"Yes, she is here to help us, and what I have to say could help, so she is at the house with the children. If they wake up, I'm two seconds away. Do you not want to hear what I have to say? Is this not important to you? Am I allowed to have any say about the fact that my marriage is falling apart?" I really didn't want to get angry, but I guess it was hard to avoid.

"Fine," he said.

I took a deep breath. "Do you not feel seen? Do I let you be yourself? Because I don't think I do all the time. I get caught up in our life and how hard it is to run it all and I start wanting everything to just fit in the right box, and when it doesn't I get angry. But that's not being tolerant. I want to be different and work with what is really there and not just what I want to be there. You know? I want to really love you through and through, good and bad, hard stuff and easy stuff, and maybe sometimes I don't? Is that how you feel? Do you feel suffocated and misunderstood? I can change," I said. (I wish sometimes I could just say one or two knockout sentences instead of twenty mediocre ones, but it's how God made me.)

"Isabel, it's late."

"Please, Josiah, is it true? Is that why you don't love me anymore?" I started to cry again.

"Look, we have been over everything. I have said everything I can think to say. We went to Dr. Bergen and that didn't work."

"But you aren't trying."

"I am trying. I have been trying for years and I can't do it anymore. I don't know how else to say it," he said, exasperated.

"Are you really not in love with me anymore?" I said. And then there was a long silence.

"No," he said. "I'm sorry."

I nodded and left him in his little office.

When I got back, Bess was in her nightgown. Our supper dishes were washed and there were two cups of peppermint tea on the counter.

"It didn't work," I said.

"Then it's Sylvia. Let's call Martin."

42

Martin was Josiah's best friend from graduate school. At our wedding he was the one who described Josiah's brain as a cathedral. Martin and his wife, Tracy, lived in Iowa, where he was an English professor. Martin looks like your average cute, scruffy college kid. He giggles and drinks beer in front of "the game" and generally doesn't strike you as the deeply intellectual, hugely successful English scholar that he is. He writes on Donne and darkness and has this gigantic brain, but you'd never know it from hanging out with him. Josiah respects him enormously. Calling Martin felt unfair to me but I was desperate these days.

"I can't call him, Bess. He's Josiah's friend," I said.

"He's Wallace's godfather. Helping save his godson's parents' marriage is part of the deal he has with God, Isabel. Get with the program."

"You call him, you're the godmother."

"Okay," she said, and she did.

I sat on the sofa in the library while she called from the

phone on the desk. The picture of Josiah, my stepson, Ian, and me was on the desk. It was taken the first year we were together at Josiah's stepmother's house in North Carolina. The three of us were on the beach. We all looked young and happy. While the phone was ringing Bess picked up the picture and showed it to me. I nodded, and she put it to her heart.

"Martin? It's Bess," she said.

They talked for a while. Martin told Bess that Josiah had called him in September to tell him about an "interesting professor who had joined the department." Martin told Josiah he didn't want to hear about it. They had not spoken since.

That was that. Josiah had wanted Sylvia from the moment she set up shop on the second floor of King Hall. Was she going to do the unthinkable? I had to find out from the horse herself.

The next day, I left Wallace and James with Josiah and drove Bess and Oliver to the airport half an hour away. We had decided before we fell asleep the night before that I would confront Sylvia the next day when I got back from the airport. In the car, Bess and I went over every little detail. How I was going to find her, what I would say to her, how I would make my exit, and what would be my cover-up for Josiah when I returned late from the airport. (I'd taken a wrong turn. Almost an impossibility as it's a straight shot from the runway to my front door, but there is one turn that I suppose if I was drunk and blind I could miss. In normal circumstances lying is stupid and pointless, as one always gets caught, but the thinking was, all is fair in love and war.)

"Okay," Bess said like a football coach, "let's go over what you say again."

"What if I cry?" I asked.

"That's okay, just be yourself. But try to be a strong self, because you do have to get the sentences out—that's why it's good you memorized them."

"Sylvia," I said to the steering wheel, "I know my husband is flirting with you. And I understand that it may just be one-sided, but if in any way you are tempted to explore the possibility of an involvement with him, I beg you not to. You know my children, you know our life. I treasure my marriage and the boys need their father. Maybe it's because you are so young or because you are not a mother that you may not understand the seriousness of this or what devastation it will cause in my children's lives if our marriage is broken up. It's beyond whatever love you two think you have." I sounded like a recording for a public service announcement urging parents to read to their kids.

"Good," Bess said. "She'll be caught off guard and you will be able to read if she's lying or not. Because she *will* deny it."

43

I dropped them at the airport and drove back to Oberlin. I was so nervous, sweating, short of breath. I am certain I was in a low-grade panic attack, but so much of my life felt like that anyway, I was able to keep driving. Sylvia's apartment was in a big white house on the edge of town. If Oberlin had a wrong side of the tracks, this was the beginning of it. It was drizzling freezing rain. I looked up at the building and discovered there were three staircases leading to apartment pockets. I didn't have much time and I didn't think I should knock on every door because the chances that I would knock on the door of someone I knew were high. My adrenaline was raging and fueling this Nancy Drew side of myself that I didn't know I had. To my right was a hall and to my relief there were mail-boxes that were open like troughs. I quickly riffled through three mailboxes without any luck and then, sure as shooting, the fourth box was Sylvia's, 3B. I ran up to the third floor. Her door was open just a crack. Without thinking too long about it, I knocked on the door.

"Sylvia?" I called.

Nothing.

I knocked again and then there she was.

She was dressed in jeans and a long, gray wool turtleneck sweater with a scarf wrapped around her neck. French people are really freaked out about drafts and often, I have found, wear scarves inside. It's pretty chic. But as I was wearing my father's dark blue L.L.Bean puffy parka and a ski hat, her annoyingly cool scarf just painted a really stark, clichéd picture of the fashionable mistress and the frumpy wife and mother. How did Bess send me on this mission looking like such a dork? We were so concerned about what I would say that we forgot the most important thing—what I would wear. I was still nursing James so my big boobs under all that down didn't help matters at all.

She did look terrified.

"I have to talk with you, if that's okay," I said.

Her apartment had almost nothing in it but a desk in the middle of the living room, books in piles everywhere, and one large modern painting leaning against the wall.

"I have nothing to offer you, I am ashamed to say," she stammered.

Goodness, I thought, the girl is always ashamed.

"Look, I just have to say something and then I'll leave," I said.

And then I said verbatim exactly what Bess and I had been rehearsing since the night before, but at the end I broke down in tears.

"I don't know what I am doing here," I cried with my head in my hands. "I'm sorry. I am so worried and frightened." She gave me a long hug and I cried and cried.

"What should I do?" she said. From her tone and the look on her face, there was an acknowledgment.

"Please, just stay away from him. Just literally move in another direction if he comes near you. Don't even look at him," I said.

I had convinced myself that she was not interested in him, but he was madly pursuing her.

"Okay," she said. "I'll do it. I wouldn't get in the way of you and your family."

"Yeah, I would hate to think what your husband would make of this." I made that up on the spot. She nodded and looked fucking terrified.

"I'm sorry you are going through this."

"Thanks," I said, and left. Mission accomplished. Now I knew that he was into her, but she wasn't into him. I felt grateful to her. So what if he had a crush. If she didn't want him then it would end, and eventually he would turn his affections back to me. Marriages weather this shit all the time.

44

When I walked in the back door of the kitchen Josiah was standing there with his arms crossed.

"Where the hell have you been?" he said.

"Were you worried?"

"No, but you have been gone for a fucking long time."

"I got lost. You know that turn at that silo-looking thing, I took it, and I got lost finding the highway again," I said, lying, lying, lying.

"Bullshit."

He knew I was lying, but how? I tell you, I didn't think that *of course* she must have called him the second I left. Why else would he be so mad at me? Why else would he be so loaded for bear? I didn't think of it because I actually believed that Sylvia was on my side. Yes, she had divulged that Josiah was flirting with her, but she told me nothing else was going on, and I believed her.

He left me alone with the boys for the rest of the day. It

was the most miserable, rainy, and cold Sunday in the history of man. I knew the boys could tell something was up. I could see it in their little faces. I didn't know what to do with them to cheer them up or convince them otherwise. I was so exhausted and so sad. We stayed inside all day and finally went to town to get pizza for supper. I had never taken them to a restaurant by myself at night. It felt weird and hard. I didn't want to be a single mother of two small children.

45

His mother came to town to try to help. She couldn't. His father came to town to try to convince him to stay. He couldn't. My parents came to town, not to try and get him to do anything, but to see the house for the first time and help me be sad. Everyone was sad. Everyone was angry. But I couldn't bear angry talk from my parents, so I made them stop. They understood, but banning their anger left them with barely any other conversation. I remember my father raking leaves in our front yard. It took him hours. His face that is usually full of light was dark and serious. He was cleaning up his son-in-law's mess and he was pissed and sad.

Sadness and anger. Those two can slow you down to an utter stop and leave you wallowing in your bed. But the sting is, you can't abandon life. Unless you don't have children or a job or friends, you just have to keep slogging along and dealing. Even though I didn't want a divorce and still believed sometimes I could stop him, prevent it, I knew I had to start the proceedings.

In Ohio there is something called a Joint Dissolution of Marriage. If you can sit down with your spouse and hammer out your settlement together, you only need one lawyer and you can be divorced in six weeks. If nothing is contested, the state can process your case really quickly and get you in front of a judge who proclaims you unmarried. Six weeks is too fast, but three years is too long, and that's what can happen if you really get into it with dueling lawyers and fighting. We didn't have the time, money, or spirit for a marathon divorce. We chose the quick, neater method.

My lawyer from Cleveland gave me a good piece of advice. He said we should come up with a separation agreement fast. If you are close to the marriage, you remember what the good parts felt like. In the beginning you both will want to treat each other well, or at least fairly. The farther you get from the marriage, the more lawyers are involved, the more he turns into an asshole he never really was before and she turns into an incredible bitch she wasn't before. Don't let lawyers talk for you because everyone will lose. Everyone loses anyway in a divorce. Both sides always have to give a little more than they want and lose a little more than they want. There are no winners.

So Josiah and I sat down at our brand-new island in our brand-new kitchen, made a pot of tea, and worked it out. Our talk was reasonable and kind. I wanted to go to New York and he agreed to that. I wanted him to make a big effort to see the kids and he said he would. I wanted some financial support although I knew whatever he gave me would never be enough in Manhattan, and he agreed.

"Will you always be my friend?" I said, crying.

"Yes," he said.

"Will you always love the boys?"

"Oh, yes."

"Will we always be their parents?"

"Always."

"I am so sad," I said.

"I am too," he said.

"Someone else will raise the boys," I said.

"You will choose someone who will be loving and kind."

"How do you know that we will be all right?"

"I just think we will be happier . . ." he said.

"You better be right."

When I was growing up my father said to me, on almost a daily basis, "Shit happens." Maybe he thought he had to remind us every day because when it did happen, as he knew it would, we were the tiniest bit ready for it. "Ohhh, this is the shit happening . . . Yeah, Dad said it would and now here it is." It happens to everybody, so the way to distinguish yourself is how you deal with the shit that inevitably will hit your fan. Sitting down with Josiah and trying to have the most painful and unthinkable conversation—how to dismantle my family—in a civilized and calm way helped me. It helps me now to know that we tried not to fight. That we tried to listen and compromise. That we tried to see each other as parents and not as wounded spouses.

But we were wounded spouses.

46

I was dreading Thanksgiving, by far my favorite holiday. Josiah and I practically bought the house because it would be such a perfect place for a Thanksgiving dinner. As late November drew near it was clear that we would not be brining a twenty-seven-pound turkey to share with our family and friends. We decided that I would take the boys to New York, where my brother and his wife and son would be, and he would stay in Oberlin. I found out that Sylvia was going home to her parents on the East Coast, which gave me the slightest bit of relief. But nothing could distract me from my misery about the fact that Josiah and I were to be separated in every way that Thanksgiving.

Josiah's mother felt so badly about everything that she paid for our tickets to go home. I knew that what was happening between her son and me was probably making her relive a very painful chapter in her own life thirty-five years earlier, but we didn't speak of it.

I was frozen with fear about going home. Even though being on a plane with an eighteen-month-old and a three-year-old is torture, I wanted the plane ride to last all the way through the following Friday so I didn't have to drag myself and my abandoned children across the doorstep of my parents' house. They had both sworn upside down and backward as the mess of my divorce was unfolding that it would be all right if I came back to New York and lived with them. The plan was to do that starting at Christmas and we were all sticking with it, but I knew that the thought of living with me and my two extremely young children was striking the fear of God into them. All dreams of quiet mornings with *The New York Review of Books* were about to be rudely dashed by an apartment overcrowded with raucous male toddlers and a broken, stressed-out single mother who had to start from scratch at age thirty-five. Not only were they distraught for me, they were worried for themselves, and how could anyone blame them?

I felt guilty and helpless. When parents turn into grandparents they will tell you that the best part is you can see the grandkids, tell them a story, and then give them back to the parents. This privilege was about to end for my recently retired parents. They were about to not be able to escape from the boys or me. My parents and I have a good relationship, but it can be wrought and dysfunctional. As much as my mother loves me, I can irritate her to no end and vice versa. We had had almost fifteen years of our own space to establish a functional, enjoyable mother-daughter relationship, but now we were being hurled backward. Sleeping four feet away from each other and sharing a kitchen. Neither one of us wanted to give up our lady-of-the-household status. But we were on the verge of being forced to. And it really sucked.

47

Thanksgiving weekend we slumped in, dropping our bags and sadness everywhere. The boys seemed much louder and more intrusive to me than they ever had. If one of them cried, I rushed them out of the room and begged them to stop. If one of them laughed too loud I cringed. If they spilled a glass of water, I acted like they took a permanent marker to the sofa. I was so tired and so frightened, and nothing and nobody was able to help me. My brother and sister-in-law were dumbfounded by my sudden turn of events and I was embarrassed by it. We spent a lot of time talking about other things. The first night we got there, after the children went to bed we all gathered in the living room for drinks before dinner.

I took the glass of white wine my father gave me and drained it in thirty seconds. I must have had three more while listening to my family talk, as my mother would say, about cabbages and kings (which means nothing). I knew everyone was avoiding the three-thousand-pound neon-yellow elephant in the room out of sensitivity to me, but it didn't help. If I could have taken my boys and gone back to Oberlin that second I would have. I hated sitting on that sofa. I hated feeling so humiliated. I hated my family and their apartment and only wanted to be at home with my husband and my children, sleeping in our own beds. But I was stuck. I was so stuck.

At dinner I was so sloshed I had no idea what I was saying. I thought I was adding to the conversation about Nora, my sister-in-law, going back to work. Finally I was excused from the table and from doing the dishes. I took an Ambien and fell asleep on the sofa in the living room. My brother and his family were in the spare room that we used to share as children.

The next day, the Wednesday before Thanksgiving, I was sitting on the floor in the living room with James, who was playing with a puzzle. Wallace was watching a video in the den. Still in my nightgown and slumped up against the bookshelf, I had reached the lowest point. My mother came in.

"Isabel," she said, and started plumping pillows. "I don't know what got into you last night, but your selfish blabbing on at Nora was unacceptable."

I looked at James, whose diaper from the night before was sagging down to his knees.

"The whole world doesn't revolve around you. I know that times are tough," she said. (Really? I thought, it sure looks like your husband of thirty-seven years is still firmly by your side, but why don't you go ahead and tell me about the tough times?)

"But if we are all going to be living here together—and

for God knows how long—you should start to think about other people and not just yourself," she said.

At that point I wished with all my might that I could just pass out. I held my breath until I could feel my fingers tingle and my face turn red. I wanted my mind to go black. It didn't. All I could think to say to my mother was "I'm sorry." I started crying.

The expression "kicking a dog when he's down" came to mind. In order for me not to totally lose it and scare the crap out of James, I had to talk in a whisper.

"Mum, my life is falling apart and I can't help it and I can't get it to stop. If you don't want us to live here, I can stay in Ohio and make some sort of life there, but as much as I don't want to move back here and interrupt your life, I think staying in Ohio as a single mother with no husband or job would be worse and may not end so well. And let me tell you, I hate the thought of moving back here. I love my life in Oberlin and don't want it to be over. I am frightened, I have no money, and I love my husband, who is leaving me. So I'm sorry if I drank too much or if I talked too much about myself. I didn't know I was doing it. I'll try and keep my head low and stay out of your way, but you have to tell me now if you don't want us."

She stiffened.

"No, Dad and I have talked about it and we are ready. We have been planning how we are going to handle it. We are resolved and I think it will be difficult at times, but we'll get through it." I didn't believe her.

48

Absence had not made Josiah's heart grow fonder of me, or at least he hadn't changed his mind about the divorce while we were out of town.

"Where did you end up having Thanksgiving?" I said.

"At Solomon's," he said. Solomon was the chair of the English department. "I felt miserable. But last night Ward and Secca took me out and that was nice."

"Was Sylvia there?" I said.

"Yes." I went cold.

Usually, my rapidly sinking heart would cause me to interrogate him further, or accuse him of loving her, or get in yet another useless conversation about him coming back to me, but I stopped myself, because I had another plan.

The next morning, a Sunday, I told Josiah I was going to the theater department to get the forms for grading. After my hitting rock bottom in New York and having very little faith in my future in general, I decided to go into all-out detective mode. I thought Sylvia was going to stay away from Josiah at all costs and I believed her. I thought she was married and had better things to do than go out to dinner in northeast Ohio with another woman's husband! But apparently I was wrong, and I was hoping beyond hope that the shy and private Secca, who had gone out for a "fun" dinner with my husband and another woman, was going to give me the answers.

I parked the car in their driveway and ran up the stairs of their very little house. It was ten in the morning and bitterly cold. I knocked on the door. Omen, their gray cat, slinked around the curtain and looked at me. I peered into their living room. No sign of life. Their car was in the driveway, but they were not up yet. They had no kids.

I pounded the door hard and waited. I was freezing. I pounded again and again and again. I felt nuts but I didn't care. Wake the fuck up and deal with me! Be accountable! Finally I saw Secca's feet coming down the staircase. I had never seen her with no makeup on. She looked at me, didn't smile, and opened the door.

"Hi, Isabel, we are not up yet," she said matter-of-factly. She didn't sound rude.

"I'm sorry," I said. "I am desperate and need to talk to you and Ward."

"Come in," she said.

We sat down in her living room on her modern sofa.

"Can you please get Ward?" I said.

"No, he doesn't want to get in the middle of this," she said.

I couldn't believe that they had talked about it. I was downstairs in fifteen-degree weather pounding on their door, and they were talking about how they were going to deal with the crisis on their doorstep? I also was shocked that they knew why I was there.

"He won't talk to me?" I said.

"No."

Another shock.

"I need to know what you know about Josiah and Sylvia."

"Why does it matter, Isabel? It will make no difference in what happens to you. Why do you want to know?" she said very calmly.

"I beg your pardon, but it makes all the difference in the world to me, Secca. If I know for sure there is something going on between them, I have a chance of stopping it. I am trying desperately to save my marriage . . . I can't believe this is happening."

She was so calm and reserved about everything I felt like I was in another world where affairs were part of the day-to-day. I was close to speechless.

"Are you not going to tell me anything? Please. I need to know," I said.

"I don't know what is really going on and I don't ask. But when we are together, it's like they are a couple. You don't come up in the conversation." She bowed her head. "I'm sorry."

I left their little house and walked down the path to our minivan. I looked up the empty street, thinking I would see the intersection where you turn into our street, but I was mixed up and looking in the wrong direction. Nothing looked familiar. I got back in the car and sat in the cold.

49

In December in Oberlin it snows lightly every day. Like the rest of the country, the town and college readies itself for the holidays. Twinkle lights go up in all the stores on Tappan Square, professors give exams, final shows go up, class parties take place, there are Messiah sing-alongs at the conservatory. Josiah and I got married in December. Our first son, Wallace, was born two years later in December. Josiah's birthday is in December. Christmas is in December. Most years it's a really good month. That year, I would have to sign my separation agreement in December, end a hopeful teaching career in December, put my dream house on the market nine months after purchasing it, and leave a life I worked so hard to build and loved with all my heart—all in December.

I didn't tell my students my life as I knew it was winding up. It was all too heavy for them to take on and it was none of their business anyway. But I did feel like a liar any time one of them would comment on our life or children.

On the day Josiah and I were going to sign our separation agreement, I insisted that we have lunch together first at Black River. We were still living in our house together, but we were seeing each other less and less. The lunch idea was in keeping with what I had been trying to do during the entire disaster. I just wanted to stay connected. At this point it wasn't even so much that I thought he would suddenly see the light and beg for my forgiveness (which I would have given him, I am positive), it was that I felt I would drown if I couldn't see him. Or maybe it was plain old denial. If we were having tuna sandwiches together at Black River, we couldn't be about to amble up the street and end our marriage of six years with Betty the bank lady, a notary. He agreed to indulge me, but he wasn't into it the same way I was. We struggled through lunch surrounded by all the students eating their first meal of the day with whatever girl or boy they had spent the night with. One student of mine, Adam, was at the table next to ours, on a breakfast-after-a-night-of-hooking-up date with some girl. Adam was from California and a big flirt. Once he put my parka on after class and proceeded to walk out the door with it on. When I called to him to give it back he came slowly, then he stood just two inches too close to me as he took it off and handed it to me, looking directly in my eyes the entire time. It was a move out of a John Hughes movie and very flattering, but all you can really do with a twenty-year-old surfer dude flirting with you is be amused and then have some big fantasy about it later on when you are very much by yourself.

Adam smiled at me. He knew I knew he had been with the girl the night before and we both thought it was pretty funny.

I tried to tell Josiah about the dynamic next to us and chatted about the plight of lovers in college and wasn't it adorable and heartbreaking. But he wasn't going there with me. He wanted to plow through this dreadful, obligatory lunch and do what we had to do at the bank. So I turned quiet, we finished, and we went to meet Betty.

Betty had also given us our home improvement loan for the William Morris wallpaper six months before. If she was surprised that we were now getting divorced, you would never have known it. Midwestern stoicism has its charms. We all three sat at the same desk and signed the official separation agreement we had worked out together in our kitchen. It didn't take long and nobody said anything. Both Josiah and I had to teach a class that afternoon. We walked across the square silently. I had the feeling he just wanted to take a different path, but there wasn't one. It's a small campus and there just aren't many ways to get from point A to point B.

"Okay," I said, looking up at him. We were standing outside of King. "I guess that is that."

"Yes," he said.

"This sucks," I said.

"Maybe there just isn't any way to have a good conversation about this now and we should just go. I have to teach."

"So do I."

"Okay then," he said.

"Okay," I said.

And I walked away. As I turned toward the theater building I noticed the clouds. They were hovering close to the ground and because of the early December light, every one was a different color. Pale grays, dark blues, whites. My eyes scanned each one, hoping that there would be a break that would allow for a ray of sun to come down. I was looking for that God light, praying some would shine on me and perform some miracle and make everything the way it was. There was none. I was about to cry or scream or run, when I saw Adam on his way to my class too.

"Hey, Teach," he said, smiling.

"Hey, Adam," I said.

"You know that girl I was with?"

"Well, no, but it looked like you two were pretty cozy."

"Yeah, she's cool." He blushed. "She thinks you and your husband and kids are the cutest thing ever, man. She went on about it after you guys left for like hours. I was like, enough already, but she's cool. She thinks your husband is hot, even though she once saw him running and he was sweating like a fucking pig."

"Yeah, the man can sweat," I said.

We walked through the snow a little ways.

"Adam, I don't want to freak you out, but Josiah and I are getting divorced. We just came back from signing the papers at the bank," I said.

I didn't feel like I was going to cry, because I had gone into teaching mode.

"I just thought I would tell you, since, I don't know . . . Don't tell anyone else in the class, I don't want everybody to get confused or . . . I probably shouldn't have told you," I said.

"Whoa, Isabel, I'm sorry, man, that sucks."

"Yeah, it really does."

"Hey, you know what? My parents got divorced when I was like eleven, and then, like three years later, they got married to each other again," he said.

"Really? How was that on you?" I said, authentically interested.

"I don't know. It's fine. I can't really remember."

"But you are okay, look at you!" He smiled. The kid tried really hard in class and he was a nice kid. I felt better about my boys.

"Thanks, Adam. I'll meet you in class," I said.

I watched him walk up the stairs of the drama department. At the door he turned around and said, "Hey, Isabel, you are going to be okay."

50

Josiah and I decided to wait until later to do the big pack. I had packed the boys' clothes, but on this day I had to pack my things. I got one of those big plastic containers from Target—the ones that are the size of a bathtub, and rolls and rolls of paper towel. I stood in my bedroom and looked around like it was the last time I would be in there. There was no evidence of Josiah. He had removed himself. It just felt like my room. The things in it were things that I loved, and most of them were doomed to spend the rest of their lives in a plastic box from Target. I wrapped the Daum green glass gorilla Josiah had given me on our wedding day and nestled it into the box. I put my wedding ring in a silver box along with the rings Josiah had given me when our babies were born. They went in next to the gorilla. There were shells we had collected from the beach in South Carolina and Polaroid pictures of us taken in bars in New York. There was a box with a set of keys to his apartment in Cambridge, and a stack of love letters tied in a brown ribbon. I cried and tried to be as neat as I could. I knew I wasn't going to unpack this box for many years. Maybe I never would. Maybe my boys would one day open it when they were men. I wanted it to look thought-through and organized. I wanted the box to be able to tell our story. It felt like the burial of a beloved friend who had died too young.

"Hey, Isabel, can I talk to you?" Josiah was standing at the door.

"What?" I said, quickly wiping my tears away.

"Did you fucking go to Ward and Secca's house?"

"Yes."

"Isabel, that was totally inappropriate," he said.

"Oh really?" The tears I had wiped away were instantly replaced. "I don't know if I would be so comfortable talking about what is appropriate or not, Josiah."

"I still work here," he said.

I just kept crying. He looked at what I was doing and his face fell.

"What are you doing?" he said.

"Packing."

"I'm sorry." He looked at me, and it was that look that is so hard to pin down. It's the look of someone who is hurting you but who loves you at the same time. It's the look that keeps me from hating him even though that's what you are supposed to do when your husband leaves you. I just think life is so complicated and subtle, and people are so different and complex and incomprehensible. He didn't want to hurt me, he didn't want to hurt the children, but he was doing it anyway, for reasons I don't understand fully to this day. He wanted something different for himself, and even maybe for us. I got it, so I just kept looking at him and crying, sitting in the middle of the things we had loved together.

"You can take anything," he said. "You can have anything you want."

I nodded and he came over and hugged me.

51

I believe in love. I believe in hard times and love winning. I believe marriage is hard. I believe people make mistakes. I believe people can want two things at once. I believe people are selfish and generous at the same time. I believe very few people want to hurt others. I believe that you can be surprised by life. I believe in the happy endings. I had a hard time believing that Josiah was actually going to leave me. The math just didn't add up. And it was going to be such a pain in the ass. Nothing was going to work well if our family wasn't living together. There wasn't enough money, there were too many miles between Ohio and New York, our friends and family would be divided and angry. It was going to be so exhausting for everyone. Who needed it?

On the last day of classes, I stopped by the English department to talk to Josiah. We had been very good to each other for the last couple of days, and it felt safe for me to waltz down the hallway and drop in on someone who officially was still my husband. His door was open when I got there and he was on the phone.

"Okay, bye," he said quickly into the telephone when he saw me. He spun his chair to face me. He was so fast to hang up the phone, I smelled a rat right away. (I was getting good at smelling that particular rat.)

"Who was that?" I said.

He heaved a sigh.

"Who was that?" I said again.

"Isabel . . ."

"Who was that, Josiah?"

He cocked his head toward the wall. "Sylvia."

I turned and walked to her door, which was locked. She must be smoking, I thought. It all was so easy. They were talking, I walked in, they hung up, she bolted outside for a butt. What did they think, I was a total moron? Probably not, I had surprised them, but didn't they know how brave I was?

I walked down the stairs and outside. There were Sylvia and Secca having a cigarette in the falling snow.

"Were you just on the phone with my husband?" I yelled. Secca darted back inside without looking up.

"Yes," Sylvia said.

"What the fuck are you doing?" I said.

Sylvia looked angry. She was wearing this military-style coat with epaulets—again, I'm sure it was Prada or Miu Miu, but to me at that moment she resembled something out of a World War II movie.

"Isabel, he is my friend. What are you so frightened of? Josiah and I will always be friends," she said, cool as a cucumber.

What am I so frightened of? Didn't she understand

that she was in the process of stealing my husband? The comment made me pause. Maybe I knew more than she did about her future. It was stunning. Maybe I knew that she was on her way to being my sons' stepmother before the idea had occurred to her. I was ahead of her, and again, there I was in my big stupid parka! But I didn't feel stupid. It's a parka that's good if you're out in the cold for a long time, like if you are in the playground with your kids. It's a parka that doesn't show dirt, and if it does get dirty you toss it in the wash. It's a coat with a lot of big pockets for sippy cups and a bag of pretzels. It's a mom coat. I felt like a mother, and mothers will do anything to save their kids. I got down on my knees in the snow.

"Please get away from my husband," I said. "We are leaving in four days and then my children will begin a life that is so unfair and mean. They love their father and they need him. And I love him and need him. Please, please, I am begging you to end whatever this is. Please."

She didn't say anything. She didn't understand what I was doing. I'm sure she thought I was being dramatic, as if there was no need for such measures as kneeling in the snow. There was a window just above us and I could feel a presence there. I looked up and saw that a long-standing tenured member of the English department was standing at his office window looking at us. He had been teaching at the college for at least three decades. He was a gentleman, old-school, respected. He had told us to buy a house in Oberlin instead of rent. He knew everything that was going on. He knew why I was on my knees. He saw a wife fighting for her husband, a mother protecting her children. Seeing him made me get up.

"I have nothing to say to you anymore," I said to Sylvia. "I will never speak to you again."

And I walked away, because it occurred to me at that moment that no matter who knew what, if he did and she didn't, or if she did and he didn't, or if they both did, they were already together and I was out.

52

Wallace, James, and I were flying back to New York on December 16. We had to leave on that day because of weird timing. But the problem was that the sixteenth was Wallace's fourth birthday and the eve of our sixth wedding anniversary. We went to New York every Christmas, so the boys did not think it out of the ordinary that we were going to Granny and Papa's, but I couldn't get up the guts to tell them we were not coming back. It was my great hope that we would come back to Ohio. I held out for the slim chance that the bad dream we were living in would be just that and we would wake up Christmas morning and there would be a telephone call from Josiah making it all go away. But as it stood, we were scheduled to go to New York without Josiah on the sixteenth and start our new lives on the seventeenth, which also happened to be our anniversary. I couldn't tell them anything about why Josiah wasn't coming with us. I was too scared and I didn't know how. So I didn't tell them anything. I just planned a birthday party for Wallace on the thirteenth before we left.

I called my friends in New York and started arranging playdates with their kids for my Ohio boys. I made arrangements to visit preschools. I accepted invitations to Christmas parties. Protective friends I had known since grade school offered to drive out there and retrieve Wallace, James, and me and all of our belongings so that we would never have to return to the town once we got to New York. I loved the idea of my old pals making a road trip to save their friend who had gone off course, but Josiah and I had already sorted out that he would drive with James's crib and the heavier essentials the day after we flew. I wanted his help and nobody else's.

53

On the very last day, we all got up for breakfast, watched *Sesame Street,* and noodled around the house like it was a normal morning. I sat on my window bench and drank tea while Josiah got James dressed in the clothes that I had laid out in the kitchen the night before. Our plane left at noon, so there was a sense of urgency, but if I had really taken in the fact that this was our last morning together as a family, no matter how broken we were, I probably wouldn't have worried about making the plane. But life keeps going and people who worry about making planes will always worry about making planes. We piled in the car, buckled up, made sure the dog was in, and pulled out of our driveway.

"Say bye, house!" I said to the boys.

"Bye, house!" Wallace chimed.

I leaned my head against the window and left the town very much as I had entered it, weeping silently so the boys wouldn't see.

We hadn't figured that we wouldn't be able to linger at

the airport. When we arrived, there were cars lined up waiting to drop off passengers, and traffic cops bustling everyone along. The boys spilled out of the car like balls; I had to collect them and keep them in one place. They didn't understand we were saying good-bye forever. Even though Josiah was driving out the next day and even though we had set up a visitation schedule, and even though we were all related, this was it, this was the last moment.

"I'm scared, I'm scared," I whispered to Josiah as I clung to his neck.

"It's going to be all right," he said. "You are going to be all right."

He held on to me tight. We held on to each other and then, because he had to, he let go.

54

At my parents' apartment on Central Park West my brother Andrew and I ate every meal (until we were big enough, seven and five, to eat dinner with my parents in the dining room) at a little painted-blue table with little painted-blue chairs in the kitchen. Our kitchen wasn't very big, but there was a perfect nook where children could eat their chicken soup with rice. When Wallace, James, and I arrived on December 16, there in the kitchen was another little blue table with blue chairs set up for my sons. Of course it wasn't the same one, but it may as well have been. I have no idea where my mother found it.

New York must have felt the same to the boys in many ways. Granny was there baking sugar cookies in the shapes of angels, and Papa took them to Columbus Avenue to pick out a tree from the people from Montreal. It must have hit them somewhere deep that their dad wasn't there and although I hate to even write this, they must have known how sad I was. My parents and I tried to put on brave faces, but it was uncharted territory and I'm not sure how effective we were. Thinking back, I probably should have told the boys the truth, that we were not going home. I just couldn't get the words out of my mouth, and I had not yet fully recognized that we were never going back to Oberlin.

This story ends happily, but telling you everything we went through after December 17 would fill another book. So I'll just tell a little and then get to the happy ending.

I had ordered a drum set for Wallace when we were in Oberlin and had it sent to New York. Although it sounds insane for a four-year-old to have a drum set in a New York apartment, it wasn't insane to have one in a big house in the middle of Ohio. I wasn't nuts, I had promised him the drum set before I knew what our future would bring. I didn't open the three boxes that the drums came in until Christmas Eve. We had all gone to the pageant at church. It's a lovely pageant that I was in as a little girl, always an angel, never Mary. It has a real donkey, so the boys were in heaven. I was taking every opportunity to get down on my knees and pray. Later we prepared a tray of cookies and wine (I know, traditionally it's milk, but in our family we leave a glass of wine for Santa), and sent the boys off to dream of sugar plums. I hauled the boxes into the living room to start the setup. My father saw this and his face fell.

"What's that? Is that the drum set?" He sounded worried.

"Yeah, I'm going to set it up so when Wallace wakes up in the morning it's all ready to go. He's going to die of happiness, right?" I suddenly felt unsure. He looked so worried and I didn't know why.

"Ish, I hate to tell you this, but I think there are going to be about seven hundred pieces in there and I'd be amazed if there are instructions." The man was speaking from almost fifty years of experience setting up kids' toys.

"Are you serious?" I frantically ripped into the cardboard boxes.

"I would love to be wrong," he said.

The first two boxes were just drums, but the third, just as Dad had warned, did have seven hundred tiny screws, bolts, and little metal rods that were necessary to keep the drums together. There was also one sheet of paper with exactly three instructions on it about how to assemble the set. I'm sure Tommy Lee would have whipped that thing together in no time, but I could tell just by looking at it that my dad and I had no chance. I put my head in my hands and cried. It was Christmas Eve and not only did I fail at producing my dear son's dad, I couldn't even manage to get the damn drum set put together to give him the slightest bit of happiness. My father read the skimpy instructions once. He folded them, put them on the table, and said, "Ish, don't worry. This is what we are going to do."

Dad had his best, most positive Plan B voice on.

"On Monday morning"—Christmas fell on a Sunday that year—"I am going to call the music store Sam Ash and pay one of those drum guys whatever it takes to come here and set up these drums with Wallace. Wallace will think it's cool that a real drum player came to set up his very own drum set. Until then, we'll just stack up these drums and hope he doesn't notice."

"He'll notice. For fun he watches footage of Neil Peart on the Internet." I sniffed.

"It's the best we can do, Ish." He patted me on the back.

Plan Bs. They are hard to swallow, but they are better than nothing, and they *are* a plan. One lesson that was starting to make sense to me was that having a plan, even if it's a meager plan, is useful and gets you through.

"Okay," I said. I wiped the tears from my eyes and started putting the mystifying pieces back into the box. I knew it was the best we could do, and the best you can do has to be enough. The lights on the Christmas tree twinkled, matching the lights of Fifth Avenue across the park. Was I the only single mother failing to assemble her son's drum set in New York? Probably not, but it felt like it.

Josiah told me on the coldest day of February that he and Sylvia were a couple. I was in a taxi and about to go to the movies by myself. I was actually going, no joke, to *The Squid and the Whale,* a movie about divorce. Everyone told me not to go, but I wanted to because I wanted to be around other people going through what I was going through, even if it was on a screen at Lincoln Plaza Cinemas on Broadway.

If I was directing the movie of our conversation, I would take the sound of me out and I would have powerful music over the picture. You would know just by watching that it was brutal, you wouldn't need words. I remember the taxi being one of those old-school checker cabs from the seventies with the little seats that folded up, but that could not have been. Those cabs were taken off the streets ages ago. Maybe I remember it that way because when I was a little girl those taxis swarmed the streets of New York City, and I felt like a little girl who was being told that her parents were getting divorced. I was never told anything so heartbreaking as a little girl. I was the adult, not the child.

He wasn't going to come back. He wasn't going to ask us back.

Plan B. Even to this day, the thought of not being friends with Josiah and not parenting our boys together in some way is unacceptable. I had to get over the fact that I didn't get to have the life I had planned for and move on.

My parents' living room looks out on Central Park. In the summer the trees are bushy and lush. You can't see the ground. But in the winter, you can see everything. You can see a horse and rider cantering around the bridal path, the runners, the dogs playing in the early morning with their owners, sipping coffee. One day I was looking out at the park. Everything was white and gray. The trees were reaching up and out, their spindly branches poking up toward the white sky. The apartment we lived in was on the seventh floor, which puts you just over those branches. Everything looked dead, but as I looked out, I thought that although everything was resting, paused, frozen, inside the earth and trees and even in the frozen reservoir there was life. I pictured myself lifting up and flying out over the trees. If I could dive into one of the points of the branches and push down into the trunk I would eventually run into the green living core, the shoots of leaves that were waiting to come out in the spring.

Wait, I thought to myself. Wait through this winter. You are strong and love life, your children are healthy, your parents love you, your friends are near. Wait and by spring you will be all right and able to grow.

My father has three rules of life he says all the time. One is Persian, something he learned when he lived in Tehran in the 1960s: inshallah. It means, "As God wills it." The next is "Chin up." That may be a Scottish thing or a sports thing. The last, and probably the most frequently used, is "Take the high road." It's a combination of all three of these and boatloads of help from everyone, including strangers, that got me back on my feet.

Epilogue

The boys have grown (they are still pretty little), have worked hard themselves, and are vibrant, sweet, good little creatures. Josiah is married to Sylvia, who is a thoughtful and kind stepmother, and it's funny, I like her now very much, in the same way I did when we first met. Josiah and I are like people who have been in a band together for a long time—we don't always see eye-to-eye, we don't even ride on the same tour bus, but we stay together because at our best, there is the music: the boys. The boys are our shared interest, their happiness our common goal.

And then I met the love of my life . . .

Acknowledgments

To my parents, because you are the greatest. To my family (*all* sides) and friends for being just that. To Sasha Lazard for the lunch in Woodstock, and Eliza Griswold for the lunch on the Upper East Side. To my agent, Bill Clegg, for his close reading, glorious mind, positivity, and most of all, for believing in me. To Nan Graham for her giant intelligence, warmth, elegance, and focus. To Susan Moldow for her enthusiastic support. To Matt Hudson and Paul Whitlatch for their good help. To all those at Scribner, who are so fantastic at getting a book from point A to point B. To the New York Society Library, a marvelous place to write.

And to my beloved husband, Peter Lattman, for your constant support, generosity, kindness, cheer, tolerance, and love.